THE SUPER CONNECTOR'S PLAYBOOK

Lirone Glikman

PASSIONPRENEUR®
PUBLISHING

THE SUPER CONNECTOR'S PLAYBOOK

How to Achieve Your Goals Through
Authentic Business Relationships

Lirone Glikman

PASSIONPRENEUR®
PUBLISHING

Thank you to the Passionpreneur Publishing team: Moustafa Hamwi, Shobha Nihalani, Scott Hurley, Tim Roberts and Cat Martindale
Photography by: Omer Hacohen
Illustrations by: Muhammad Abdullah

The Super Connector's Playbook
Copyright © 2025 Lirone Glikman
First published in 2025

Print: 978-1-76124-208-3
E-book: 978-1-76124-210-6
Hardback: 978-1-76124-209-0

Because of the dynamic nature of the Internet, any web addresses or links contained in this book may have changed since publication and may no longer be valid. The information in this book is based on the author's experiences and opinions. The views expressed in this book are solely those of the author and do not necessarily reflect the views of the publisher; the publisher hereby disclaims any responsibility for them.

The author of this book does not dispense any form of medical, legal, financial, or technical advice either directly or indirectly. The intent of the author is solely to provide information of a general nature to help you in your quest for personal development and growth. In the event you use any of the information in this book, the author and the publisher assume no responsibility for your actions. If any form of expert assistance is required, the services of a competent professional should be sought.

Publishing information
Publishing and design facilitated by Passionpreneur Publishing
A division of Passionpreneur Organization Pty Ltd
ABN: 48640637529

Melbourne, VIC | Australia
www.passionpreneurpublishing.com

To my mom, Sima, may her soul rest in peace, who taught me to love people and always look at the good, optimistic, and magical side of life; and my father, Arie, who showed me the world and how to connect with the people in it and enjoy the journey.

Table of Contents

Foreword –
Dr. John Demartini

In today's interconnected world, building authentic, meaningful, and sustainable relationships is crucial for both personal and professional achievement and fulfillment. Lirone Glikman's *The Super Connector's Playbook,* offers a groundbreaking approach to networking, rooted in over twelve years of research and extensive practical experience. Her methodology, emphasizing the 'human factor', provides effective strategies for cultivating genuine and powerful bonds that can propel you toward your most inspiring and meaningful goals.

Lirone's insights resonate deeply with my philosophy that your highest values and authentic connections unlock and actualize your true potential. Throughout my career, I have seen the transformative power of genuine relationships. *The Super Connector's Playbook* is more than a guide to networking; it's a comprehensive blueprint for building and engaging your network through authentic communication and sustainable fair exchange, helping you navigate your endeavors with greater ease, influence, and fulfillment.

What sets this book apart is its actionable advice and the focus on authenticity. Lirone's tried-and-tested techniques are designed to optimize each personal connection, ensuring your relationships are not only beneficial but also fulfilling. Her insights, gained from her journey in applying the *Human Factor* Method, will help you gain essential support for achieving both personal and professional goals, turning the daunting task of networking into a rewarding journey of personal growth.

I highly endorse *The Super Connector's Playbook*. Lirone Glikman has created a valuable resource that will undoubtedly transform how you build and maintain relationships, enabling greater achievement and fulfillment in all areas of your life. Prepare to embark on a transformative journey with Lirone as your guide.

Love & Wisdom,

Dr. John Demartini
World-renowned human behavior expert, international bestselling author of *The Values Factor*
www.drdemartini.com

1

TURN THE WORLD INTO YOUR OYSTER

Why networking is the skill you must master to live a fulfilled life

"Opportunities are rarely offered; they're seized."

— SHERYL SANDBERG

Y ou can achieve anything you want through the power of relationships.

Do you remember yourself as a child full of dreams? What did you want to be 'when you grow up'? What type of adventures and achievements did you envision for yourself?

Not everything we want to be as children truly happens, but that doesn't matter. What matters is that we know we have the ability and power to get there, to try and make it happen. It gives us a sense that there are no limits to the kind of life that we wish for. This book is designed to help you achieve the life you want.

From frustrations to finding my biggest superpowers

My story, exploring the world of relationship-building ('networking'), began when I was a little girl from a small village, with many global dreams ... and some struggles. At first glance, I probably wouldn't have seemed like the type to have a difficult time making friends. I was that friendly kid who was *too* eager to meet people. When meeting new people, I was always fun—and perhaps even a little 'pleaser' in some people's eyes. In my optimistic view of the world, being ultra-nice to others would automatically earn me their love. But I actually felt misunderstood at times, having many shallow friendships rather than deep and strong ones. I felt that other kids didn't know how to read me and accept me for who I was.

Yet I still always owned my fundamental characteristics: my big smile, my positivity, and my passion to influence others. Even if the people around me didn't 'get' me, I was sure that my way was right for me, so I kept exploring it. I ignored the doubters and hung on to pursuing my dreams of success—and my life changed when I began taking steps toward realizing them.

At age 16, I was full of enthusiasm and big ideas, ready to take on the world. I knew that to fulfill my dreams, I had to take the first leap. That was the only way forward.

I wanted to work in the media field so I could impact more people positively. So, with Mom and Dad's encouragement, I arrived at the local radio station 90FM and boldly knocked on the CEO's door, even though I was nervous and expected rejection. I was direct, honest, and passionate when I asked if I could work for him. The CEO, Aharon Orgad, was stunned by my confidence. He didn't throw me out, which I took as a positive sign. In fact, he listened to everything I said. After thinking about it for a few minutes of stressful silence, he said: 'OK, you can produce a show twice a week for $30 per month.' In that very moment, he saw potential in me and recognized my genuine desire to get that job. I was thrilled! It was in that instant that I realized that if I could knock on a CEO's door and ask for a job, I could do anything in life. This single brash request turned out to be one of my defining moments.

THE SUPER CONNECTOR'S PLAYBOOK

Although I was offered a tiny salary to cover my commuting expenses for producing the top-rated show on the radio, I saw that as a fantastic deal. Aharon was the first person I encountered in my professional world who wholeheartedly *believed* in me, giving me the confidence to excel. I gave this job all I could and I wanted to do more.

Just one month later, I approached Aharon again, asking if I could 'open a microphone' and report on a local event. Why did I take the risk of asking for another opportunity? I figured that I had come this far, so why shouldn't I ask for a step up?

He gave me that same knowing look; he knew I was capable of doing it. It was his 'go for it' attitude that seemed to give me an edge and motivated me to do my best. The decision promptly turned me into one of Israel's youngest radio broadcasters.

A few years later, still hungry for more, I ventured into TV, marketing, and PR. I wanted to work in global companies and as the daughter of a commercial airline pilot, I was eager to pursue an international career and travel the world.

Learning through experiences
I had many career aspirations that I wasn't able to fulfill. There were countless moments when I became deeply frustrated. I felt isolated from opportunities because I didn't know how to

get past the closed doors; coming from a small village, I didn't know how to find the person who'd open them for me and give me a chance to reach my dreams.

This deep pain and dissatisfaction led me to start asking myself many questions, observing others, researching, reading, and examining ways to excel.

Some of the questions I raised were:
- Why do some people succeed in building relationships, while others don't?
- What makes a strong connection?
- Why do my friends hear about opportunities that I miss (whether socially or work-related)?
- What do 'popular' people do to be welcomed everywhere they go?

I observed many people around me

I worked in television with celebrities and began to understand how to distinguish what's fake from what's genuine. Behind the scenes, I heard a lot of phony talk, but I also saw people form genuine bonds that led them to more opportunities.

I observed my friends, discovering that I didn't appreciate some of them enough, while valuing some who weren't necessarily there for me. This helped me learn that good friends are there through thick and thin, helping each other from the heart.

Through observing my interactions with siblings and parents, I came to realize what a role model my dad Arie is when it comes to networking. He has friends from every profession and his stories and sense of humor make each conversation an adventure. My dad's a magnetizing person; people love to be around him and support him. And my mom, Sima (rest in peace), had the ability to connect with people from the heart—from a deep, loving, and accepting place that also made people gravitate toward her and remember her always.

I started to investigate

I read every book I could find, including *Never Eat Alone* by Keith Ferrazzi, *Power Networking* by Brian Tracy, *How to Win Friends and Influence People* by Dale Carnegie, and more. I mingled with and interviewed businesspeople, ambassadors, and international experts like networking guru Dr. Ivan Misner, learning how they network with different people or work the room at events. I also took much inspiration from the path of businesswoman and author Arianna Huffington, the business and life approach of entrepreneur Marie Forleo, and the insights of human behavior expert Vanessa Van Edwards. I examined and absorbed every piece of information about networking that resonated with me.

Then, at some point I got it! I figured out how to do it!

So, how to network for results?

First, you need to understand that it's about acquiring different skills:

- How to build a wide network
- How to present yourself correctly
- How to authentically connect with others
- How to be a connector of others
- How to leave a lasting impression
- How to get results from your network
- And many more.

My brave move: From theory to real life

I decided to test my findings. It couldn't be done on home ground; I had to be in unfamiliar surroundings and practice the lessons I had learned. This was going to be the test that would prove I had a method I could follow (and later, teach). It was exciting and nerve-wracking, but I knew I had to take a leap of faith, because you can't achieve your dreams while staying in your comfort zone.

With a resilient spirit and passion, armed with my learnings, I moved to Sydney, Australia alone and started from scratch. Of course, many close friends tried to talk me out of it by saying, 'Nothing is waiting for you there but kangaroos.' Yet I had nothing to lose, and the dream of working globally was strong enough to outweigh any fears. I gave myself the chance to apply what I'd learned about relationships, build a network of people from zero, and reinvent myself in a place where no one knew me. As the saying goes, 'A change of place brings a change of luck.' I wanted to live the Australian life, but I didn't know anyone there. With only a suitcase and a work permit, I began networking from scratch, implementing all that I'd learned.

Those 'superpowers' I mastered started to work faster than I'd hoped, and within two weeks I found a job in a jewelry store in Westfield Shopping Center in Bondi Junction. One day a customer, Daniel Arixi, came to the shop. You never know how a random person you briefly met can become significant to you, and so it was for me. While chatting, he asked me what brought me to Australia. I responded: 'I have experience in radio, marketing, and TV. I want to do the same here.' I was direct, honest, and transparent. Daniel was a bar promoter, and all he could do was to offer me a job in a bar. Seeing it as the perfect way to expand my network and meet many new people, I accepted. And so it was—he opened the door to a whole new world of great people to connect with.

While working in the bar, I noticed that I was encountering the same nice guy everywhere I went. We frequented the same Bondi Beach bars and restaurants; I even saw him on the streets we both walked all the time. One day, I decided to take the initiative, asking him his name—and why we were always at the same places but hadn't been properly introduced.

He said his name was Eddie Wong, then asked: 'What brought you to Australia?'

I replied: 'I have experience in radio, marketing, and TV, and I want to do the same here.'

Eddie, who later became a life-long close friend of mine, offered to connect me with Ben, the manager of Bondi 88FM radio, where he was broadcasting as well. I was meeting with Ben and sharing my experience with him when he told me something I'll never forget:

'You know, your English sucks but I love your vibes and I'm going to give you a radio show here!'

It was unbelievable!

There I was, a broadcaster with a show every Tuesday from 2 to 4 p.m., speaking in broken English, but with an unstoppable, contagious enthusiasm! Honestly, with the bad English I had then, even *I* wouldn't have given myself a show. That's a life lesson I carry with me: Many times, it's less about your skills than your vibes. People are drawn to fun, energetic, radiant individuals.

Come with the right vibes, and doors will open for you! Within one month of landing in Australia, I had a radio show, while bartending at night, working at the jewelry store in the mall in the daytime, and enjoying a flourishing social life, forming close friendships.

Two months later, I met someone who introduced me to a businessman who was impressed by my experience. Soon enough, this wonderful man gave me a job at Westfield Shopping Center's Headquarters in their marketing division, as a campaign assistant supporting the 20 Westfield Shopping Centers across Australia. All this happened by meeting the right people and opening the right doors with authenticity, ability, and assertiveness.

The interesting part is, this was the headquarters of the shopping center where I worked at the jewelry shop. Incredibly, within three months I had been promoted from a seller at a shopping mall store to the marketing division of the whole chain! As time passed, I could see how much I'd progressed. What I did there wasn't just luck—it had also come from a skill I'd mastered.

Superpowers Revealed: The *Human Factor* Method

I returned to the books I'd read and continued to research and take stock of my experiences. Through them, I developed a methodology, the *Human Factor* Method, for achieving goals through authentic relationship-building. Before long, word of my expertise spread and I was invited to major events as a speaker, writing for international magazines, and developing my dream business, where I could share my recipe for fulfillment with others.

With my global dreams pushing me to take greater action, I decided to test my method again. I wanted to go for it big time, so I moved to Manhattan, New York! This time, I was smarter—by following my method, I landed a job in just *three weeks.* The *Human Factor* Method worked again! I got a job in a Manhattan-based PR firm, gained experience, expanded my network, and leveraged my connections to get clients to host workshops for bodies like eBay and Cornell University. I even became an honorary advisor to a UN-affiliated NGO committee.

This story demonstrates that anything is possible. Many doors can open up for you when you master the power of relationships!

Take that leap into YOUR fulfillment

Often, we pay too little attention to the people around us— including how they can help us connect with our goals, just as we can help them with theirs. Yet relationships are the key elements that enable us to achieve what we want and live a fulfilling professional and personal life.

You can't achieve anything without the help of others, so developing the skills to authentically bond with anyone and cultivate relationships is crucial.

'But we communicate with people all day, so what's new?' you might ask.

You're right!

We know how to communicate, but not necessarily how to leverage the human capital around us towards our own fulfillment and that of others. This book will provide you with the blueprint nobody else shows you—how to achieve your goals through relationships and networks, first and foremost authentically, but also strategically.

This book focuses on the **business world**. That includes finding a job, growing a business, fundraising from venture capital, and getting a promotion, up to effectively managing projects within organizations. It's also relevant to your **personal life**: finding partners, getting a good deal on a home, moving and adapting to a new place, and more. It's all about knowing how to plan and materialize the connections with the people in your life, authentically.

Everyone aspires to achieve goals, both big and small, but not everyone is aware of the profound impact that relationships can have on leading a fulfilling life. The primary reason? We haven't been taught how to leverage our relationships effectively.

Time to open your eyes to endless possibilities

My journey began from a place of frustration, lacking the connections and avenues to grow professionally as I wanted. However, the *Human Factor* Method has given me unique superpowers and an international network that lets me reach countless people and companies, work with them, and impact their future with my methodology and experience. It's also allowed me to fulfill my dream business and life. Through this journey, I've collaborated with major organizations worldwide, establishing connections with international experts and renowned figures—individuals I once only dreamed of having as part of my life and network. Through learning, testing, refining, and experimenting with my methodology over decades and succeeding in unfamiliar territories, I've found my path to self-fulfillment.

If I can do it, so can anyone!

Since 2011, I've had the honor of teaching and sharing this knowledge worldwide—in over 26 countries on five continents, helping countless people from myriad backgrounds with the *Human Factor* Method.

People have told me that my method has changed the way they approach others to make connections. At the same time, their confidence and understanding of how to build relationships have improved, because they finally had a blueprint to follow. They share how quickly they've found a job, how easily they've attracted clients, or how they've developed the ability to maintain relationships with people they used to be afraid to talk to. These experiences have inspired me to commit to helping people take the initiative and build authentic relationships toward their fulfillment in any field.

Here are some examples of how the *Human Factor* Method has helped others achieve various business goals:

- **If you're looking for a job**, you'll want to hear what Alon Kichin told me: *'You opened my mind to what's possible. I researched and worked on it as you guided me, and found a job.'*

- **If you're at a conference and want to create better connections**, Jacob Refaelov says: *'For me, you're a mentor, an inspiration. I learn much from you and when I implement it in conferences, I connect well with the right people and see the results.'*

- **If you're looking to break into the international market**, Viki Glam, Co-Founder of Enerjoy, says: *'[Lirone] taught us how to initiate connections from scratch in the international market and fulfill the project's vision and bring my product to the world's leading companies.'*

- **If you want to build a brand that attracts customers to you**, entrepreneur Meir Yaniv shares: *'Lirone turned me into a superstar online. She gave our company global recognition that helped us with our sales and expansion.'*

- **If you want to scale your business**, Meital Shamia, Global Programs Manager at Microsoft for Startups, says: *'Lirone is a regular speaker and highly regarded mentor at Microsoft's startup programs. Her knowledge of networking strategy, experience in entering new markets, and expertise in building brands have helped our companies scale. She always inspires and teaches practical tools.'*

- **If you want to learn how to network better at your organization**, Dudy Bar-Tal from Google says: *'The reason we found Lirone as a qualified speaker for Google Campus is due to her phenomenal experience as a global expert in business relationships.'*

- **If you want to inspire your team to take action in networking and drive results**, Yotam Sharan from the eBay office in New York says: *'Lirone provided practical and crucial tools around relationship-building and branding within the company. Lirone demonstrated an extremely knowledgeable and professional approach and engaged eBay employees to take initiative!'*

Everything in life is about relationships and connections

When you start networking authentically and strategically, you'll notice a shift. It's a shift that grows over time, strengthening your ability to connect with others in a genuine way. This will gradually create a life in flow, where you have everything you want available to you, and where you're able to reach any result or solution or just gain support through a quick phone call with people you've been authentically connected with over the years.

I'm going to unveil my *Human Factor* Method in the following chapters. With it, we'll begin to explore how we meet people and interact with them. Before we do the deep dive, though, let's address a few important considerations and dismiss some common fears. Ready?

2

UNLEASH YOUR INNER NETWORKER

Let's uncover your hidden connector power!

*'Life's greatest rewards are reserved for those who
demonstrate a never-ending commitment
to act until they achieve.'*

— ANTHONY ROBBINS

In this chapter, you'll learn the foundations of building relationships. Networking is an important skill, yet it has developed a negative reputation. People 'love to hate' it. When the word 'networking' is being thrown around, many reject the idea because it is considered to be fake or not the appropriate way to progress in life. These are limiting beliefs. There are so many fears related to networking:

- The fear of rejection
- The fear of coming across as annoying
- The fear of being seen as manipulative
- The fear of making a fool of oneself
- Or even the fear of taking initiative and failing (or succeeding).

Networking is your superpower for fulfillment

Think about our lives and the many people we interact with. Anything we need or want in life depends on other people. Throughout human history, we've survived and thrived through networking, communication, connection, and collaboration with other people.

Professor Yuval Noah Harari, the noted historian and philosopher who has researched the history of all humankind, has stated that all of humanity's success is due to collaborations:

'Humans control the world basically because we are the only animals that can cooperate flexibly in very large numbers.'

Everything we want to achieve—whether it's to do with your job, finding the solution to a problem, finding love, or gaining a sense of belonging—we can only achieve through the support of other people from our network. And when you think about it, we didn't come into this world because of one person; Mom and Dad wanted to collaborate to get us here.

Let's try to understand in this chapter why we 'love to hate' networking instead of realizing its power to shape the reality and life we want to live.

What is networking?

It surprises people when they realize how simple networking is as a concept, yet it is not easy to implement. It's essentially the creation of genuine connections, giving to others, and enjoying the interaction.

That, in essence, is what draws people to others and helps them form true bonds. I like to put it this way: Networking is a way to go from A to Z quickly and reliably—and to enjoy the journey.

Networking helps us fulfill our lives through the power of connecting with others. It can increase earning potential and create a social safety net. Networking allows us to enjoy unique experiences, influence others, or simply build honest and courageous friendships. To make this work, we must be *authentic* in our approach and help others achieve their goals.

Giving value is the currency of networking. It starts with being a giver, offering connections, resources, time, and information. When you are able to help others, you become memorable to them. It's like the personal blueprint that you leave with everyone you meet. Once you understand this, you can implement it confidently in your interactions.

So if networking's so beneficial, why do people 'love to hate' it?

One reason is that most people are afraid to network with people they don't know. Let's normalize it; we all have social fears. According to public speaking statistics, 90% of the population reports some level of shyness and anxiety in social interactions. This made me feel much better when I first read it, because it normalizes the fear of social interactions. We ALL feel uncomfortable, yet we're all wired to form connections.

This is going to be shocking—ready?

What if I told you that you're already a networker?

Think about it. When has it worked for you? Many times, I'm sure. It could have been when you've approached a girl or a guy, started a conversation with a stranger on the street, or asked for help from a distant acquaintance.

What was it about these interactions that led you to succeed? Courage? Belief that it would work?

To further normalize it, let's think about our experiences. If you've ever had any of these thoughts when meeting new people, check the box next to it (I'm sure you've had at least one):

- ☐ 'They probably don't like me.'
- ☐ 'I just said something so stupid.'
- ☐ 'Maybe I'm annoying them by approaching them.'

Now that we understand we all share some social fears, remember the root reason why we love to hate networking is simple yet crucial: *We're not formally taught how to do it.* But I can help you break out of those limiting beliefs.

I invite you to take a moment for self-reflection to shed light on how you network.

EXERCISE

Let's see what's holding you back and identify when you've already acted as a networker.

1. Write down three fears that you have about networking.

    a. _____

    b. _____

    c. _____

2. Think of a very important goal that you simply *had* to achieve, one that made you develop the courage to see it through.

    _____

    _____

    _____

3. Write down two instances where you successfully created a connection that led to meaningful results, then describe the goal that motivated you to take action in each case. (Example: I asked a distant friend to recommend me for a job at their company, as my goal was to secure employment.)

    _____

    _____

    _____

We are biologically wired to create connections

It was discovered that our biology is intricately linked to our social behavior. Hormones such as oxytocin, often referred to as the 'love hormone', play a crucial role in fostering connections and bonding between individuals. When we engage in acts of kindness, cooperation, or simply listening to others, our bodies release oxytocin, promoting feelings of trust, empathy, and bonding.

This biological mechanism suggests that, as humans, we are naturally inclined to seek out social connections and form relationships with others. When we overcome the initial fear or hesitation associated with reaching out to someone, whether it's initiating a conversation with a stranger or asking for help, the release of oxytocin reinforces positive feelings and satisfaction.

Also, the act of offering assistance or support to another person not only benefits them but also activates reward centers in our brains, leading us to value and cherish the connection we've made. This reciprocal nature of human interaction highlights our innate desire for social connection and the emotional fulfillment we derive from helping others.

Overall, our biological predisposition to seek social connection, coupled with the emotional rewards of empathy and altruism, underscores the fundamental importance of relationships in human life. By understanding and embracing this innate tendency, we can cultivate deeper connections, foster empathy, and enrich our lives through meaningful interactions with others.

Introducing the *Human Factor* Methodology

The roadmap to create enriching connections that will transform your life includes the following components (which I'll go into in more detail later in the book):

1. **Goal setting:** Establishing clear objectives that you want to achieve, to fulfill your needs and dreams.

2. **People planning:** Being strategic about whom to connect with, so they can help you achieve your goals.

3. **Personal branding:** Crafting and showcasing your unique identity and value proposition to the world, online and offline, in a magnetizing way.

4. **Connecting:** Actively breaking the ice, connecting and fostering meaningful, authentic relationships, and leaving lasting impressions with almost anyone you meet.

5. **Maintaining relationships:** Nurturing and sustaining ongoing connections over time with the right people for you.

6. **Leveraging for results:** Harnessing your network authentically, to help you achieve tangible outcomes and desired results.

Lirone Glikman's 'Human Factor' Methodology
Achieve your goals through relationship-building

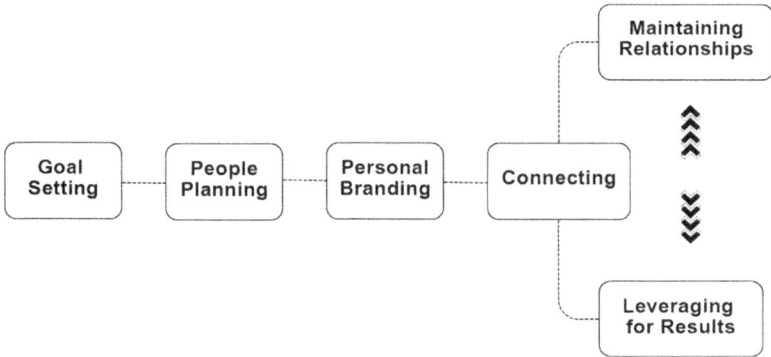

One of the reasons that networking has a negative reputation is that we attribute it to fear and rejection. On the other hand, our bodies are wired for making connections—but only if we put ourselves out there. It's crucial for you to learn how to do this correctly and in a way that suits you.

In the following chapters, we'll dive into the method with practical tools you can use immediately, supported by case studies and real-life stories of how I have used them.

Before that, though, I have one very important request when you read this book. In every chapter and with every tool, ask yourself: 'How can this work for me?'

You need to find your way to make what you learn benefit you—to adjust it to your way of thinking, your words, your feelings, your industry, and your own reality. Think how you can connect the tools to the situations you find yourself in, whether it's in the work environment or in your private life. What are the attitudes required for your field of work? Whom are you talking to? Are they a manager or a subordinate? Asking such questions is the way to get the most out of this practical book and the *Human Factor* Method.

In the next chapter, we begin with defining your goals and what they mean to you. Let's dive in!

3

AIM FOR YOUR DREAM GOALS

Uncover what will make your life and career fulfilled

*'Everybody has their own Mount Everest—
we were put on this world to climb.'*

— SETH GODIN

I n this chapter, you'll develop a slightly different perspective on your goals, whether they're small or big. We'll focus on the reason you want them. The more you truly desire them, the better it will be for you to get out of your comfort zone and connect with people to achieve them.

In this chapter, we'll be looking at these topics:

1. **The power of desire meeting opportunity**
2. **The challenge of understanding what we want**
3. **When your purpose meets your passion**
4. **Identifying your own goals**
5. **Using your goals as your motivator to thrive.**

The power of desire meeting opportunity

Imagine your future.

How will you feel every morning when you wake up? Who will be beside you in bed and in your home? What will you do for a living? What are your hobbies? What are you proud of? How do you feel about the impact you're making on others?

Now I'll ask you: **Why** do you want this future?

How will you feel and who will you be when you achieve the small goals that make up this picture of your future?

Being connected to your *'why'* is a powerful mindset. It's your engine to build connections and step out of your comfort zone. This is because achieving your professional and personal goals starts within you. You start by driving action, then continue by creating momentum through your communication with people—and the result is fulfillment. You should believe that such results will come into your life.

How can I say this so confidently? Read this carefully: Research shows that people who genuinely believe they are lucky actually succeed more, because they are *aware of and open to identifying opportunities* more than others—and you can be too! Richard Wiseman, a psychologist, conducted research that revealed a connection between people's beliefs about luck and their actual experiences. His findings suggest that individuals who consider themselves lucky tend to notice and capitalize on opportunities more than those who believe they are unlucky. This mindset influences their behavior, making them more open to possibilities and resilient in the face of challenges. Essentially, Wiseman's research supports the idea that a positive belief in one's luck can contribute to a self-fulfilling prophecy, influencing life outcomes.

You can be this way too. Since opportunities often come through people, it's important to be aware of how those you meet can help you reach your goals. Also, remember the value you can offer them—and how you can be a 'lucky star' for someone else.

How my goal met opportunity and became my reality

Do you remember I told you that as a little girl, I had many global dreams? One of my dreams was to become involved at the UN and influence representatives of the world's nations to work towards a better world. This goal was always on my mind, waiting for the opportunity to materialize.

In 2015, just a week after I moved to New York by myself with a big dream to make it in the Big Apple, I was invited to a friend's birthday party at a nice bar, just next to Union Square. There, as I mingled with people, I saw this man in a suit, sitting on the sofa. He looked very serious, but I could see that beyond that image there was a person with a big heart. A minute later, the birthday boy introduced me to him: 'This is Isaac Reshad; you guys should meet.' We had a nice chat, connected, and laughed. He told me about his work and mentioned that he was involved with the UN in a committee that works towards Sustainable Development Goals ('The SDGs'). My eyes widened in surprise; I knew that was the moment when my dream had met with an opportunity!

My radar screamed 'Opportunity, opportunity!' And I had to ask. So I did. 'Hey, that's interesting because I always wanted to work for the UN, and I believe I have much to contribute.' He said: 'Tell me more, like what?'

So, I shared my professional background and what I could offer. Isaac took my number and said he would contact me the next day. Honestly, I wasn't sure that he would really contact me, but he did. The next morning I got a message from him: 'Hey, let's talk—I need some more information from you.'

After a few weeks of interviews and screenings, I became an honorary advisor to the NGO Committee on Sustainable Development – New York, an affiliated United Nations NGO committee. I've been there ever since, advising, speaking at their events, and connecting with ambassadors, global NGOs, and similar entities to support the achievement of the UN Sustainable Development Goals. I made it work out!

By the way, Isaac is still a close friend. I keep good people close to me in my life's journey. This is a great example of the truth that everything we want happens through people. I know this from my own life, but I also like to search for academic evidence that backs up my experiences: LinkedIn has found that referrals are the top source for finding a job or clients. Also, in 1987, Peter V. Marsden found that people with a larger core discussion network tend to access more diverse views. This increases their chances of achieving personal and professional goals, like finding a job or clients.

In conclusion, opportunities are all around us. When you know what you want—your small needs or big goals—you become more aware of the information and people around you, and how they can serve you and your goals. When your desires meet an opportunity, what should you do? Ask for it: Make sure the other person understands what you want. This is how you start momentum, how you get closer to achieving what you need and living a fulfilling life.

The challenge of understanding what we want

Do you really know what you want to do in life? If your answer is 'yes', then you are lucky. If your answer is 'no' or 'not sure', that's OK too—keep working on it.

Research shows that our values, our self-concept, and society's expectations influence us. These factors often lead us to doubt our personal desires and fear judgment, making it difficult to be open about what we truly want. This creates a complex situation that challenges our self-discovery process and hinders our ability to identify our genuine desires.

Taking time to reflect, seeking advice from professionals, and understanding what we want in our personal and professional lives can help us get there. There are moments in life when we find that what we'd wanted no longer resonates; this might be because we've achieved it, or we've got over this need, or we've simply reached another stage. While it may feel like we're 'lost' or 'damaged' if we don't know what we want, I applaud those moments because they prompt us to sit down again, think hard, and figure out what we truly want. When you define what you want and set your goals toward it, you'll be ready to achieve them.

Embrace the journey of self-discovery and networking; it's a powerful combination that will lead you to achieve your true desires and goals, while surrounding you with people who care and want to see you thrive. In the following pages, I will guide you on such a path.

When your purpose meets your passion

In 2005, I was living in Sydney. One sunny day, on my morning walk down Curlewis Street in Bondi Beach, I was listening to the Bon Jovi song 'It's My Life' over my headphones (the jazz version by Paul Anka) when I experienced a Eureka moment. I realized, as if I was downloading information to my brain, that my purpose in life is to help people fulfill their lives through the power of relationships.

BOOM!

Now, this moment came after many days and nights and years of struggle and self-examination. I had spent a lot of time using the Japanese 'Ikigai' framework that invites each of us to examine what our abilities are, what we love and are good at, and how we can serve the world with them. It all came down to that *'Aha!'* moment when my life path became clear.

My passion was always about getting to know people, learning from them, observing their behavior, discovering how they think and act, and understanding how we can find common ground and connect. I have always seen the power of real connection as sacred. A bond with someone is a gateway to mutual support, to actions that can change the world. I have always felt alive, loved, and growing when I socialize with people. It energizes me like no other activity.

That's why *my purpose* fits so perfectly to what I am good at and love. My desire to help people fulfill themselves through the power of relationships is my big 'why'. It's the reason for writing this book and teaching people globally.

Passion and purpose

Passion and purpose are the two pillars that support our inner sense of fulfillment. When you align with them, work becomes a joyful activity, and there is an innate motivation to push one's potential, to achieve purpose.

Now, what's the difference between passion and purpose?

- **Passion** is the 'what' we want.
  It makes us ask: 'How can it serve me?'

- **Purpose** is the 'why' we want it.
  It makes us ask: 'How can I serve the world?'

EXERCISE

Define your passion and purpose by answering the following questions, inspired by the Ikigai framework.

Passion ('What': 'How can it serve me?')
Questions:

a. What specific activities or endeavors bring you immense joy and fulfillment?

_____
_____
_____
_____
_____

b. In what ways can your passion contribute to your personal growth and well-being?

_____
_____
_____
_____
_____

c. How might embracing your passion enhance your overall
   life satisfaction and happiness?

_____

_____

_____

_____

_____

Many leaders have suggested some of the signs that indicate
you are living your passion:

- You lose track of time while working ('flow state')
- Your results are excellent
- You inspire others
- You have no need to explain or convince others
- You know what you're doing.

Purpose ('Why': 'How can I serve the world?')
Questions:

a. What values or causes resonate deeply with you on a global
   or societal level?

_____

_____

_____

_____

_____

b. In what ways do your skills and interests align with making a positive impact on others?

_____

_____

_____

_____

_____

c. How can you integrate your purpose into your daily actions or work to contribute meaningfully to the broader community?

_____

_____

_____

_____

_____

Studies indicate that recognizing and living your life purpose leads to a higher sense of happiness and satisfaction with life.

Once you answer those questions, take time to reflect on the main questions of the Ikigai framework: what you love doing, what you are good at, what the world needs, and what you can be paid for. Give yourself the time you need, and you will gain more clarity about what you want to do and why you want to do it.

And once you get clarity... pursue your passions and fulfill your purpose.

Identifying your own goals

Whether you are a startup founder, self-employed, or employed by a company, understanding your professional goals is very important. It not only provides clarity on your desired career path but also helps you identify the key individuals who can assist you in getting much closer to reaching them.

By defining your goals, you gain insight into the skills, resources, and connections needed to succeed, allowing you to pinpoint potential mentors and collaborators, as well as other networking opportunities that align with your aspirations. Building relationships with individuals who possess the knowledge and experience relevant to your goals can provide invaluable guidance, support, and opportunities for growth.

Additionally, fostering connections within your industry or community can open doors to new possibilities and enhance your professional development journey. Therefore, it all starts with defining your professional goals. Doing so shapes your career trajectory, while enabling you to cultivate a network of individuals to help you navigate and thrive on your chosen path.

EXERCISE

Define your goals.

Here are some examples of long-term and short-term goals:

Personal goals
- **Short term:** Improving work-life balance and spending more time with family.
- **Long term:** Pursuing hobbies I have always wanted to explore.

Professional goals
- **Short term:** Complete a leadership training program within the next 12 months.
- **Long term:** Become a senior manager or director in my industry within the next 3–5 years.

a. Define your personal short-term/long-term goals:

_____

_____

_____

b. Define your professional short-term/long-term goals:

_____

_____

_____

Goals Matrix

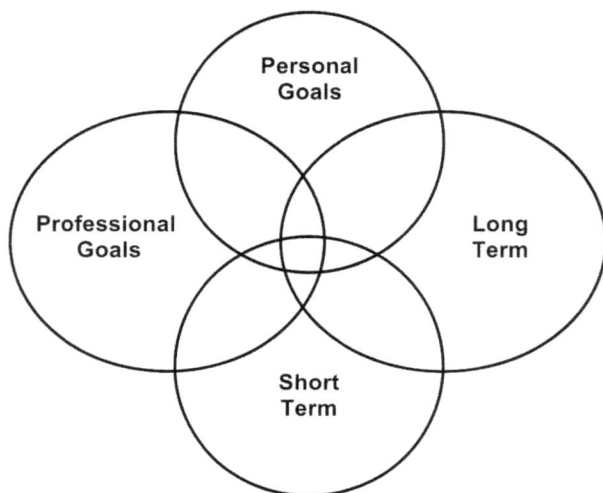

Your network can support you in many ways—just as you can create value for them. Below are some common professional needs and how mutual support can help you achieve them.

1. **Client outreach**
   - **Your goal:** Connect with potential clients or partners.
   - **Your network support:** Leverage your network for introductions, referrals, or insights into potential clients.

2. **Skill enhancement**
   - **Your goal:** Develop or enhance a skill relevant to your business.

- **Your network support:** Seek recommendations, online courses, or mentorship from your network to aid in skill development.

3. **Productivity focus**
   - **Your goal:** Prioritize and complete key tasks efficiently.
   - **Your network support:** Share and exchange productivity tips, tools, or accountability with your network to stay motivated.

4. **Market research**
   - **Your goal:** Stay updated on industry trends and competitor activities.
   - **Your network support:** Engage in conversations with industry peers for valuable insights and market intelligence.

5. **Marketing efforts**
   - **Your goal:** Promote your business through marketing channels.
   - **Your network support:** Seek collaboration opportunities or gather feedback on your marketing strategies from your network.

6. **Networking within the company**
   - **Your goal:** Expand your internal professional network.
   - **Your network support:** Attend internal events, engage in cross-departmental collaborations, and seek mentorship within the organization.

Try to alter how you view any small need, desire, or goal by matching it to people and roles that can help you achieve them. This new pattern of thinking will surely help you identify many people who can support you. In the next chapters, you will learn more about how to identify these individuals and willingly harness their support.

Using your goals as your motivator to thrive

A goal or a need can be so important that it makes you automatically motivated to achieve it. You become your own motivator to approach other people and make it happen. The condition is that you must step out of your comfort zone to achieve it.

Remember, we are meant to live lives of fulfillment, and that can only happen when we get off the couch. When I first left everything behind to go to Australia at the age of 22, I told myself I was 'traveling to places I've never been, to achieve things I haven't yet achieved,' and so it was!

My next big adventure was moving to New York City. I had a goal I was deeply passionate about: I wanted to make it big time, and they say that if you can make it there, you can make it anywhere. The first step was getting a job and establishing a supportive network, so I systematically applied my *Human*

Factor Method and found a job in New York in three weeks, with only a small network of people.

When you know the goal, it becomes easier to identify the opportunities and people who can help you. Here's how I used my model to achieve my goals in New York:

1. **Goals**
   - **Short term:** To find a job in New York in my field of expertise, and to create supportive social circles and gain international job experience.
   - **Long term:** To build my training company and help people fulfill themselves through networking.

2. **People planning**
   - **Short term:** To find a job, I aimed to meet people in the field of marketing, set meetings, and ask for introductions to such people from each person I met.
   - **Long term:** I got to know speaking and training agencies and companies in New York to collaborate with them in the longer run.

To expand on that, I leveraged my network to arrange meetings with agencies, asking each contact to introduce me to two more people, which exponentially grew my connections. I documented everyone I met in a mind map app and Excel sheets. With this expanding network, I scheduled 5–6 meetings daily until I secured the job I wanted.

THE SUPER CONNECTOR'S PLAYBOOK

3. **Personal brand**

   I shared my story about my experiences and my dream to make it in NYC with everyone I met. However, I updated and tailored my story to each individual I spoke with to appeal to them in the best way, and I also aligned the main messages on my social networks. Basically, I shared my professional compatibility and experience in marketing, PR, and media across Israel and Australia, while touching their emotions with my dream of working in New York.

4. **Connections**

   Using my 'Small Talk' formula (see Chapter 6) and my way of building genuine rapport with people, I connected quickly with almost anyone. I had a ritual: I conducted research on everyone I met with; I was genuinely curious about them and talked with them about what was important to them and the common ground we shared; and I created a connection and harnessed it by genuinely discussing my dream and how they could help me achieve it.

5. **Maintained relationships**

   I made sure to follow up on everyone, helped where I could, requested support, updated them on my progress, and kept many of these connections as my friends for the years to come.

6. **Leverage for results**

   I asked specifically for what I wanted—a job in my field. Eventually a friend from Australia introduced me to her

US partner, who hired me to work in a PR company in NYC. After almost 100 meetings within three weeks of landing in the USA, I had myself a job.

And… mission accomplished!

That's how I used the *Human Factor* Method to achieve my goals in a new place with a small network.

EXERCISE

Analyze a role model.

Consider the people in your life and choose someone who is great at achieving goals and can serve as a role model to you. Reach out to them and learn how they identify opportunities that lead to success.

_____

_____

_____

_____

_____

Visit my website to download the workbook for *The Super Connector's Playbook*, to excel in your networking and take your professional and personal life to the next level. Visit: www.lironeglikman.com/TSCPworkbook

Scan me

The bottom line

Success is often connected to the strength of your desire for the goal. When you know what your goal is, you become open to opportunities. However, this won't work for you if you don't put in the effort. Change your perception about achievement and your ability to attain it: Start seeing the world as your oyster and every person as a potential friend who wants to help you.

Begin with one small step to reach out to someone who could be the one who will change your life or current circumstances. It's in your hands to make it happen; nobody will do the work for you. And once you grasp that concept, it's easier than it seems.

Now, let's work on how you can strategically build an authentic network.

4

CRAFT YOUR ROADMAP
TO ACHIEVEMENT

Get to know your network
like never before

'The most connected people are
often the most successful.'

— KEITH FERRAZZI

What is a 'people plan'? The same way that companies have a marketing plan or a business plan, you should have a people plan. Let's learn how to form one.

These are the fascinating topics we'll cover in this chapter:

1. **Understanding the science of networks**
2. **The method for planning your network of success**
3. **Where to find the people you want to get to know—online and offline**
4. **Blueprint for building new connections**
5. **Using generative AI tools to plan your network**

Understanding the science of networks

Networks of relationships are organized within a set of rules, believe it or not. We understand by now that we can achieve almost anything we want with the help of other people, but most of us don't know how to build or create a network of such people because we are not taught how to do so. If we knew, we would get closer to our goals.

Fear not!

Let's talk about the science of networks. I will show you that you probably already know and have good access to the exact people who can help you achieve any goal—but you may not see them as such valuable contacts.

Let me introduce you to 'Dunbar's number'

The Dunbar number, proposed by anthropologist Robin Dunbar, refers to the cognitive limit on the number of people with whom one can maintain stable social relationships. This number, often cited as around 150, suggests that our brain has a finite capacity for managing social connections effectively. Thinking about the Dunbar number can be incredibly valuable in daily life, as it highlights the importance of prioritizing and nurturing meaningful relationships. Understanding its implications for networking can revolutionize how you approach building and utilizing your social connections and the results you can bring instantly into your life.

Have you ever had one of those moments when you suddenly remember that you know someone who could have helped you in a time of need? I'm sure the answer is yes! Perhaps you forgot about the acquaintance who works for Amazon; you could have consulted them when you applied for a job there. Or even the neighbor's kid who's good with computers and might have saved you from having to take your laptop in for repairs.

If you want to live a life where the answers to all your needs and problems are right in front of you, get to know your network!

Have you heard of the 'six degrees of separation' concept?

Six degrees of separation is the idea that each person is six or fewer social connections away from anyone else. As a result, a chain of 'friend of a friend' statements can be made to connect any two people in a maximum of six steps. It originated in 1929, was popularized by the social psychologist Stanley Milgram in the 1960s, and even became a type of game when in 1994, three Albright College students—Craig Fass, Brian Turtle and Mike Ginelli—invented the game that became known as *Six Degrees of Kevin Bacon*, which encouraged people to find a way to reach the actor with a maximum of six people.

According to the dynamics of networks, outcomes often come from the third and fourth circles, as these are the people who are usually exposed to information that is not accessible to you. While outcomes can occasionally arise from your first circle, especially when you're entering a new market or country, the most significant opportunities typically emerge from the third and fourth circles. Therefore, it's crucial to understand how to reach people who can expose you to a new world of knowledge and opportunities.

The question to be asked is: How can you get to know your network in a way that maximizes its potential for your success?

EXERCISE

Creating a mind map.

This is a powerful one to reach contacts from different circles. Start to create a map of your connections that relates to your goal. For example, let's say you are looking for a job at a Fortune 500 company and trying to reach someone in their HR department.

1. **Goal setting:** Write the person/title you wish to reach in the center, such as 'HR in Fortune 500 companies'.
2. **Branch out:** Create circles for aspects of your life: Community, Family, Jobs, LinkedIn, Social Media, Volunteering, Travels.
3. **Fill in details:** List the names of people you know under each aspect that is related in some way to HR in Fortune 500 companies. Example: 'Community – Beth (Google), Jenny (Amazon).'

Start to create a map of your connections that relates to any decision-maker that can help you achieve your current goal.

By visually mapping out your network, you'll activate your brain's ability to recall the relevant people you know who are most likely happy to help if you just ask. Doing this mind map exercise will make it easier to identify your relevant contacts effectively. Give it a try and witness the transformation in how you engage with your network.

Mind Map Your Network – Example

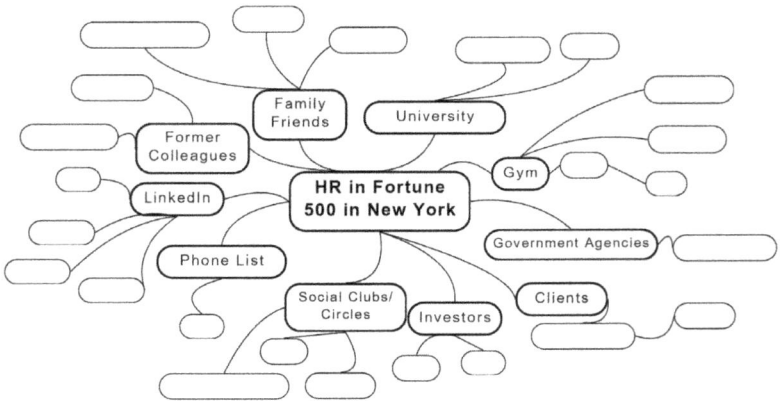

Remember:

- Networking takes time. It requires patience, and that's a reason why people may not like it.
- Don't be mistaken about this: You *don't* remember everyone you know.
- There are many people around you who are just waiting to help you—if you only ask them for help.

Now you know how networks are structured, and you can start planning your own.

The method for planning your network of success

How to plan your network is not something we have been taught. People think it's so manipulative to approach others with an agenda, but nothing in the world is created without an agenda behind it. Therefore, a people plan is needed to get to where you want to be.

How did I come to plan my network? Since I was a little girl, I've traveled the world with my father, Arie, a commercial airline pilot. Whether it was to China, the Netherlands, South Africa, or New York, everywhere I went, I was fascinated by the people I met and their rich cultures. I would ask countless questions about them, and from a young age, I learned just how interesting and diverse people are around the world. I've always had this burning desire to build a network of diverse friends and acquaintances from all over, because it gives me a sense of belonging and security to know that I'm loved and accepted anywhere and to really feel like the world is my oyster. It's driven me to understand people's customs, how they think, and what they love, as well as to gain access to business or social opportunities. Twenty years later, this vision has become my reality. Today, I have the privilege of teaching this around the world to people who want to gain a similar sense of belonging and opportunities wherever they go.

So what is a good network?

A robust network is characterized by its diversity and wide-spread connections. It encompasses a variety of individuals from different backgrounds, industries, and perspectives. It thrives on a broad reach, extending across various social circles, professional communities, and geographic locations.

By incorporating diverse voices and spanning a wide range of connections, a strong network offers access to valuable insights, opportunities, and support, enhancing personal and professional growth.

Men networking vs. women networking

How do you network? Studies suggest that gender differences in network-building reflect societal norms and individual preferences. Understanding these nuances can inform more effective networking strategies for both men and women. Let's explore the science that can make you more aware of how you build your network.

- *Men* often prioritize larger, more diverse networks that emphasize professional connections and social status (Eagly & Wood, 2012). They tend to prefer networks that offer access to resources and opportunities for advancement and are mostly comfortable pursuing these connections to gain results (Gould & Fernandez, 1989).

- *Women,* on the other hand, tend to focus on smaller, more intimate networks centered around personal relationships (Cross & Madson, 1997). They emphasize reciprocity and trust, cultivating networks based on mutual, emotional and social support (Ibarra & Andrews, 1993). They prefer nurturing these relationships and are generally less inclined to ask much from their networks.

This suggests that men's networking style typically involves building widespread networks and actively seeking direct access to opportunities, while women's networking style tends to focus on smaller networks, prioritizing deep, supportive relationships before seeking anything in return (if at all). Food for thought.

EXERCISE

How do you form your network, and how can you enhance it? Consider factors like the size of your network (vast vs. small) and the strength of your connections (strong vs. weak).

_____

_____

_____

_____

_____

Cultivating a network is a skill that can be developed over time. Once you understand the logic behind it, you're on your way!

The people strategy of President Bill Clinton

As described by Bill Clinton himself in his autobiography, during his days as a Rhodes Scholar at Oxford University, the 22-year-old adopted an interesting habit that caught the attention of his peers. He was often seen walking around campus, engaging in conversations with fellow students while diligently jotting down notes in his notebook. Curious about this behavior, an older student approached Clinton one day, seeking to understand the purpose behind his continuous note-taking.

'What are you writing about everyone here?' the student asked.

Clinton responded with a confident smile, 'It's simple. I have a goal. I'm determined to become the governor of Arkansas.' Clinton figured that to achieve that, he needed to start by identifying and connecting with the right people who could support him on this journey. From trustworthy peers to those who shared his political ideologies, from individuals with diverse skills like marketing prowess to those born into influential families or with financial resources, he mapped out a network of allies who would stand by his side as he pursued his ambitions.

Years later, as we know, Bill Clinton realized his goal, rising to become the governor of Arkansas and eventually serving as the 42nd President of the United States.

From Clinton's story, I extracted a 'networking people strategy' that emphasizes clarity of purpose and strategic relationship-building:

1. **Have a goal:** Clinton's determination to become the governor of Arkansas provided direction for his networking efforts.

2. **Identify potential allies:** Recognizing the importance of supporters, Clinton carefully identified individuals he connected with and who could contribute to his aspirations.

3. **Map your network:** With a clear understanding of his objectives, Clinton strategically mapped out his network, pinpointing those who could aid him in achieving his political ambitions.

4. **Approach and engage:** Armed with a well-defined network, Clinton approached and engaged potential allies, harnessing their support and forming alliances to bolster his campaign and eventual success.

Bill Clinton's journey serves as a great example of the power of goal-driven networking in achieving one's aspirations.

EXERCISE

Run 'Clinton's People Strategy' for a specific goal you have:

a. **Define your goal: What** do you aim to achieve?

_____

_____

_____

b. **Who** are the individuals you want to connect with?

_____

_____

_____

c. **Where** can they be found?

_____

_____

_____

d. **How** will you motivate them to connect and assist you?

_____

_____

_____

This formula for planning your network can come in handy— if it helped Clinton win the presidency, it can definitely help us.

Where to find the people you want to get to know—online and offline

Knowing what we want is one thing, but finding the people who can help us is like searching for a needle in a haystack. *How do you find them?* This is an important question, because you save time and hustle when you do it right. Let me show you how to do your networking efficiently.

Mapping contacts: Utilize tools like mind maps to scan and organize your network to find decision-makers and contacts who can help, as previously explained in this chapter.

Your network lobby: This is a powerful method to surround yourself with key people who want to and can support your journey. Compile a list of your 'lobby' of individuals, people in your network who have one or more of these qualities:

- Knowledge
- Connections
- Prestige
- Money.

These people can usually open doors for you. You know they are around you, so identify them and ask them to set a time when you can share your aspirations and see if they can support you. Your lobby can include these types of people: businesspeople, experts, lawyers, CPAs, mechanics, clients, colleagues (past or current), trade organizations, media reporters, academy professions, 'super-connectors', former seniors, community managers, etc.

Your Lobby of Super-Connectors

Write down 5–10 people you want in your lobby.

_____

_____

_____

_____

_____

Power circles: We all have our power circles, which are sometimes referred to as our 'hidden networks'. I am a part of many groups on WhatsApp or social media where people are happy to help each other just because they are a part of the same group. Thanks to these groups, you can aspire to reach a stage where you can access almost anyone's information, or that of someone close to them. Can you imagine how much simpler that makes life? How much quicker it is to make connections? It also gives you a sense of trust and security, knowing that no matter where you are, you can reach people who might want to help you.

These are the superpowers that power circles give you! Leverage the fact you are a part of different social circles, such as:

- University alumni networks
- Parents of your children's friends
- Sports teams
- Former workplaces
- LinkedIn or WhatsApp professional communities
- And more.

The shared identity within these circles serves as a trust accelerator, fostering a willingness to help one another.

Write down 2–5 circles you should explore to find people relevant for you.

_____

_____

_____

_____

_____

Increase luck: There is a way to increase your chances of meeting the right people you are seeking: by hanging out where they do. Consider places that your desired contacts frequent, such as volunteering for specific NGOs, or attending industry, charity, or gala events, gyms, your industry's go-to restaurants, co-working spaces, private social circle or union events, or theme-based WhatsApp groups. These are opportunities to serendipitously meet the influential individuals you are targeting, connect, and potentially bring luck into the achievement of your goals.

Write down 2–5 places you will go to increase your chance of meeting relevant people.

_____

_____

_____

_____

_____

Fantastic! By now, you surely know how to find any decision-maker or person within your network.

Blueprint for building new connections

There's a famous quote often attributed to Irish poet William Butler Yeats: 'There are no strangers here, only friends you haven't met yet.' This is how I view the world. Some people may seem to have a big brick wall between themselves and strangers. People don't want to approach them, for fear that they may get rejected, but you can break down the walls between yourself and any stranger if you choose to do so. Going out there in the world and seeing it as a kind of game—one in which you need to find the right 'buttons' to press to get other people to open up to talking to you—is actually fascinating!

To get to know strangers, and get them to help you, it's always preferable to be introduced by someone you know. This is the strongest, most reliable form of connection and it feels the most comfortable to a stranger. Asking someone for a referral is requesting an introduction that occurs indirectly. The main mistake people make when asking for a referral is *not* telling their contact exactly what to emphasize to the third person in order to capture their request in the best way. Remember to do this next time you ask for a referral.

We don't always have a personal connection to someone though, right? So we need to 'cold call', reaching out to someone who doesn't know us and doesn't necessarily have the motivation to answer us. The possibilities for reaching people today are endless. We can find almost any person through an internet search or by using social media search engines or other networking platforms. Yet with all these possibilities, there's still a problem: Many people just won't answer your email.

I've researched this topic and done some of my own experiments. A study done in 2018 by SpamLaws.com shows that over 14 billion spam messages are sent on a daily basis globally. That means 45% of all emails are spam!

So how can you be a part of the 55% that *aren't* considered spam?

Simple: You need to ensure that your emails/messages build your **credibility** and are **interesting** enough to attract the recipient's attention. No one really teaches us how to do this. In most cases we copy our peers, learning from experience and trial and error. That's why I crafted a workshop session and an eBook with a list of 21 ways for cold reach-outs that drive responses. I have tried and perfected these methods countless times with success, and I use them to train others to get responses. You can download the eBook on my website: www.lironeglikman.com.

How else can you approach strangers?

Here is one of the best sequences of actions I use:

1. **Search for the relevant person** (e.g., a regional marketing manager at Salesforce). Conduct online research to find out how best to connect with them on both professional and personal levels.
2. **Like/comment** on their recent LinkedIn post so they will see your name and associate it with positive communication.
3. **Send a connection request linked with a friendly note** or compliment (serious or playful), such as: 'Hi David, I'm using Salesforce and thank you guys every day for creating

such a remarkable tool, so happy to connect!' Alternatively, send an email (text will follow).

4. **Call to action:** What do you want to happen next? A meeting? Sending your CV? Aim there!

Remember this cold message formula:

- Keep it short
- Make it personal
- State your reason for making contact
- Establish credibility
- Spark interest
- Include a call to action with a question mark at the end (which is estimated to increase chances of response by approximately 20%).

Example for a text for LinkedIn or an email

(Adjust as needed but keep it short.)

Hi David,

Nice to e-meet you. I enjoyed learning from your post about Salesforce marketing strategy, and I noticed that May Green is a mutual connection. So, I took the liberty to reach out to you.

I would appreciate the opportunity to consult with you regarding a Marketing Coordinator position at Salesforce.
My name is Jane Smith, and I have five years of experience in marketing management with global companies, and have collaborated with companies such as ASICS, Microsoft, and more.

Could we schedule a brief call?
Thank you in advance!
Jane

Now adjust this to your needs and try it out!

Using generative AI tools to plan your network

Solutions based on Generative AI (Gen AI) tools have become a great companion to the way we plan and manage our relationships, but it cannot and should not fully replace us. We must keep the 'human to human' connection; that's the personal strength we have, more than any AI can do for us. You can use all kinds of Gen AI text tools to write your messages and content, but always remember to proofread the results to ensure that it represents your original purpose faithfully.

When it comes to planning your network to achieve your goals, you can use Gen AI text tools to help you identify relevant people and determine how to approach them by sending a cold message based on my formula.

Here are examples of relevant prompts you can use (customize to your needs):

1. **Prompts to get ideas for people you should connect with:**
   Use this prompt to adjust to your needs.

   a. **Guidance to identify relevant professionals to connect with:**
      'I would like to work in a [role + sector].
      My work experience is [share your work experience and strengths or personalize the answer].
      In such a case, what types of professionals should I connect with to gain insights into the industry, relevant skills, and potential career paths?'

   b. **Ask for insights from a specialist's perspective:**
      You can also ask the text tool to provide answers as if it were a specialist in a specific profession, like a CEO of a biomed company or an HR headhunter:
      'Answer this question as if you were Steve Jobs (or any other figure).'

2. **Prompts for researching and crafting a cold message**
   Use this prompt as a guide and adjust it to suit your needs.

   a. **Start with your professional experience:** Begin by sharing your professional background with the Gen AI text tool. Ask it to reflect on your description to ensure it understands what you do.

b. **Provide information about the person you want to approach:** Next, tell it about the specific individual you want to approach, for example, *'The CTO of a company called Wix.'* Share information about the CTO so it will be able to personalize the message—what the company does, along with key information about the manager. For example, copy and paste their LinkedIn 'About' section or any data from their profile or elsewhere online; feed the text tool with relevant professional and personal information you can find about them.

c. **Ask the text tool to personalize the message:** Then, ask it to personalize a message for your purpose and adjust it as needed, using this prompt that follows my cold message formula:

'Compose a message to [Person's Name + a personal hook that can spark a connection].

You are reaching out to [seek consultation/send a CV/request a call]. [Share your relevant background].

Utilize the following formula when crafting the message:
- *Keep it short*
- *Make it personal*
- *State the reason*
- *Establish credibility*
- *Spark interest*
- *End with a call to action, including a question mark.'*

d. **Experiment with the different text tools:** Find the right tools and approach that work best for you, and tailor your messages to the people you are reaching out to.

How to reach any person and get them to engage with you

I used to work in the sports tech industry, where my role involved building relationships with seniors in global sports brands and federations worldwide. We hosted a basketball innovation exhibition at the University of California at the same time as the NBA All-Star weekend in LA, knowing that all media and senior basketball leaders would be in the city then. My task was to attract sports reporters to our tech exhibition, hoping they'd be keen on exploring emerging basketball technology amidst such a major event.

The biggest challenge was that NBA stars are way more interesting than emerging basketball technologies!

I meticulously mapped out sports media and reporters in the LA area. Using a personalized approach on LinkedIn, I crafted compelling messages. I made sure to highlight common ground and offer intriguing stories, rather than simply making requests like everyone else. Leveraging name-dropping with respected figures, I effectively positioned myself and our event. Of the 30 reporters contacted, I received around ten responses. I talked with all of them, trying to sell them our stories. Two reporters ultimately attended our event, resulting in three articles—one of which was published in *USA Today.*

I achieved precisely what was needed. This experience exemplifies the impact of crafting the right message, pressing the right 'buttons' to engage the right person, and ultimately reaching our goals.

This is one of the LinkedIn messages I sent:

Hi Brianna,
Nice to get connected as we both share passion for sports, but are you into sports innovation?
I would like to set a call with you and learn what stories would interest you?

We are hosting a basketball innovation exhibition and competition in LA alongside the NBA All-Star weekend, which might interest you.
Our company represents the most amazing startups that are transforming the world of basketball and sports.

<The company> is a platform that connects countless sports tech industry leaders, working closely with brands (NBA, Google, Adidas, Microsoft, Sky Sports).

When are you free for a call?
Cheers, Lirone

Feel free to share your results with me via LinkedIn.

Visit my website to download the workbook for *The Super Connector's Playbook*, to excel in your networking and take your professional and personal life to the next level. Visit: www.lironeglikman.com/TSCPworkbook

Scan me

The bottom line

I want you to reach a stage where you can pick up the phone to call the exact someone to assist you at that very moment. As I mentioned, you have so many people who can help you with almost anything you may need in life. (Just as you are there for them.)

To get there, you need to know your network. This step of building your people plan is super important—it's the network strategy, and a strong one allows for good positioning and implementation. If you skip this step, you'll waste valuable time networking without meaningful or timely results. This plan creates focus and efficiency. I promise it will pay off, bringing you confidence and success.

Now, let me ask you a question: Once you have identified relevant stakeholders, found them, written a compelling message, and even sent it to them, what is the first thing you should expect?

Exactly! They're going to try to understand who you are. They may Google you, look at your LinkedIn page, and do their research on you just as you have done yours. This is where your personal branding comes into the picture. It can elevate you to the heights of success and open doors for you—but it can also induce people to ignore you and move on.

I'd like you to craft your authentic, magnetizing personal brand to make these stakeholders happy to hear from you. In the next chapter, I will teach you how to do this.

5

THE POWER OF YOUR PERSONAL BRAND

Your brand can get you 'in or out of the door' just like that!

'Your personal brand is the single most important investment that you can make in your business (and career).'

— STEVE FORBES

In this chapter, you will learn how to design your personal brand to convey your authentic attributes to the business world; then you will learn the best ways to build awareness of that personal brand. Here's how we'll do it:

1. **The power of your brand to get you in or out of the door**
2. **Why does your brand matter?**
3. **Discovering your personal brand**
4. **Build awareness of your brand**
5. **Build your offline brand—through your actions**
6. **The simple art of crafting your online brand**
7. **Key points for building your personal brand**

The power of your brand to get you in or out of the door

Let's play a word association game. Write the first association that comes to mind when you see or hear about these people:

- Beyoncé _____
- Mark Zuckerberg_____
- You_____

Yes, you! What association comes to people's minds when your name comes up? (This may be a tricky one…)

Now, consider this: When decision-makers google you, will they find the information you *want* them to know about you? The key word is 'want'—what do you want them to learn about you?

We all have a personal brand, an image that we put out there to the world. Some manage it consciously, enjoying its fruits, while others do not. The key here is awareness of your brand and taking the necessary action to express your authentic image.

Your brand is that secret sauce, your extra edge that yields more results! It's the promise you share about who you are and what it's like to work and interact with you. A personal brand is crafted to elevate us in all areas of life, projecting an authentic image that radiates credibility and builds trust.

So, how can your brand assist you in achieving your goals?

a. Getting your needs met
    • Getting support from colleagues easily at work
    • Getting others to happily connect you to stakeholders
    • Getting uncommon personal/professional requests answered positively
    • Being able to count on others to be there for you.

b. Fans who advocate for you when you're not present
    • Choosing you for a project or promotion
    • Sharing appreciation and acknowledgment of you
    • Recommending you as the go-to person.

The formula to become a people magnet

The more value you provide, the less effort you need to put into building and maintaining your network—others will ensure they reach out to you.

Your brand is a significant component to help you connect with people and garner their support in reaching your goals. Your brand can open or close doors without you understanding why you got the job or client—or, on the other hand, why no one returned your call. According to a national research study conducted by Brand Builders Group, 82% of all Americans agree that 'companies are more influential (and they would be more willing to buy from them) if their executives have a personal brand they know and follow.' This statistic emphasizes the importance of a brand, even if you're an employee and don't own the company.

Why does your brand matter?

In the realm of products, brands are tailored to specific audiences. When you think of Coca-Cola, what's the first word that comes to mind? What about YouTube? These words represent the brand attributes, the impressions you've gathered through interactions with these brands—i.e., they can be 'fun', 'tasty', 'bad for you', 'good for you', or more.

Similarly, in the professional world, we promote ourselves to a targeted audience. The questions you need to ask are:

a. **What are you promoting in yourself?**

What traits and messages do you want to emphasize in your professional 'hat'?

_____

_____

_____

_____

_____

b. **Who is your audience?**

Who are you speaking to? Often, it can be different audiences—your employees, your bosses, industry stakeholders, suppliers, headhunters, and investors. List them all.

_____

_____

_____

These are important questions that I recommend you think about deeply.

Remember, we all have 'brands'. Now, let's dive into crafting your authentic brand identity.

Discovering your personal brand

You already have a brand, but most of us don't take the time to break it down and become aware of what we truly convey. You are a person full of strengths, values, and skills. In this section, you will see what you project and determine if it aligns with the aspects of yourself that you want others to see.

EXERCISE

To help reveal your authentic brand identity, I'll guide you through shaping the foundation of your personal brand. Let's begin with some key questions.

AI TIP

To complete this exercise, you can also open your favorite Gen AI text tool and start a conversation. Tell it about yourself first, as preparation for your next question. Share your professional background, achievements, and aspirations. Copy your CV in and press 'Enter'. Then ask it to help you answer the questions below.

---

a. **Identify your professional goals**
   What are you striving to achieve? Define your career objectives to anchor your personal brand, as brand expression is

a way to support achieving those goals. (You can use your answer from Chapter 3 on goal setting.)

_____

_____

_____

_____

_____

b. **Define your values**

Ask your closest colleagues about the top three values steering your work ethic. Also, write down what *you* think your top three values are. Then, choose the top values and list those that characterize you the most.

_____

_____

_____

_____

_____

c. **Recognize your distinctive strengths**

Quiz those colleagues about your three distinctive strengths at work. Also, write down what *you* believe your top three strengths are. Then, choose and list the strengths that characterize you the most.

_____

_____

_____

_____

_____

d. **Craft key messages**

Determine the two key messages you want the professional world to know about you without a doubt. (For example: I'm the go-to person in my field; I know how to make any project a reality.)

1._____

_____

2._____

_____

When considering your brand, remember the role that indirect, non-verbal elements play. Think about the ways you are representing your values/strengths/messages through:

- your clothing style
- your energies
- the tone of your voice
- your email/messaging communication style.

Now, look at what you've written—this represents the essence of your personal brand identity and should reflect your authentic self in the professional world. Aim to convey these messages, values, and strengths consistently and genuinely, both in person and online.

Build awareness of your brand

Your brand exists both online and offline. I encourage you to Google your name in an incognito window to get an objective view about your online brand. You want to get a look at how you're being seen by those who search for your name.

Make sure to search your name in the language or variations that other clients, stakeholders, or recruiters might use. Examine all results—images, videos, news, etc.

Ask yourself: How well does this information align with the messages you *want* to convey?

_____

_____

_____

_____

_____

- If it aligns perfectly, fantastic!
- If it aligns partially, identify areas for improvement.
- If it doesn't align very well, it's time to build that brand.

By the way, the findings of such a search can be interesting. You might find childhood photos or discover people with the same name. There is no right or wrong here, but you have to know what it says about you, so you'll be responsible for your online brand. That's why it's always good to run a Google search about your name from time to time. Adjust or change content to make sure your online image is congruent with your messages and the authentic image you wish others to see. Next, you'll learn more about how to do it.

Build your offline brand—through your actions

How do you craft your brand? It's easier than you might think. It's all about consistency in your messages.

Consistently conveying your top messages, values, and strengths shapes the brand, both in person and online. I'm a smiley person. If you see me smile every time you interact with me online or face to face, then you know it's probably authentic to me. The same is true about knowledge around a topic, about values that are important for us, and so on. What you emphasize becomes a part of your brand.

After establishing what your brand identity is—how you authentically want to be seen in the professional environment—communicate it to the world.

Understanding how your brand is perceived, through feedback from friends and those Google results, you may experience a *gap* between the parts of your identity you want to show

THE POWER OF YOUR PERSONAL BRAND

(values, strengths and messages) and the ones that actually exist. This is where you should take actions, online and in person, to emphasize your brand identity's messages in a planned and authentic way.

Actions can shape your brand and there are many you can take. Here are some examples to consider:

- **Initiating or participating in company initiatives:** This will put you out there, getting people more familiar with you and reminding them what you can bring to them and what you stand for.

- **Mentoring and supporting new employees:** This action can emphasize different strengths, such as leadership, professionalism, being a 'people person', and more.

- **Sharing information or a unique perspective in meetings:** You want this to align with your messages.

- **Attending social events and sharing insights:** You can convey specific messages and values through your posts and publications by sharing relevant insights from events you've attended.

- **Volunteering:** This will emphasize more social-related attributes of your brand.

EXERCISE

Contemplate your offline brand identity, your actions, and what you convey. Then, consider how you can enhance your *actions* by 5% to better emphasize your brand values, strengths and messages and align them with the ones you want to highlight.

_____

_____

_____

_____

This is the type of question we rarely ask ourselves. Take this opportunity to explore how to grow your influence and expand your potential.

The simple art of crafting your online brand

Based on the 'Google yourself' exercise results, when people Google you, do they find the information you want them to know about you? (Remember, Google isn't necessarily on your side. It has no special strategy for you; it just shows what it sees online. That's why you should know and manage online information about you.)

What messages, strengths, and values do you wish to emphasize to your professional audience? With this question in mind:

- Start reviewing your social media channels to ensure you are sharing a consistent message about yourself. Unify tag-lines and messages across the networks (profiles, photos, details).
- Post frequent content that highlights your messages, values and strengths.
- Always strive to give value to your readers through your posts.
- Repeat.

When posting, start small

Many people either don't like to post on social media or are not sure how to do it right. You don't have to post daily; a minimum of 1–2 times a week can work well to build your brand. Choose a maximum of two platforms, such as Instagram, LinkedIn, a personal blog, or a company blog—select only those you can manage and that your audience engages with. Begin by being consistent with repeatable content anchors. For example, publish a relevant article every Wednesday and add a few words of your own opinion, or every Sunday, share a personal story that evokes emotion and connects to your messages, or post a case study from your industry.

Building your online authority

There are many types of content, but here are the ones that will establish your authority over time:

- **Narratives and case studies** of well-known brands and companies, demonstrating market insights and showcasing your knowledge.

- **Quick tips or quotes** with simple yet valuable information related to your field of expertise.

- **Articles** you've written or articles from reputable magazines with your added commentary. Sharing content from influential figures in your industry helps associate their brand with yours.

- **Summary of events or courses** you attended with actionable key insights, e.g., '3 things I learned working with the tech market in Taiwan that you should know'. You want to be able to tag as many relevant people as you can.

- **Ritual content**, for example, a weekly post acknowledging people who made a difference during the week.

EXERCISE

Write your social media action plan.

a. Which network are you going to work on?

_____

_____

b. What ritual content will you use?

_____

_____

c. What two other types of content will you use?

_____

_____

Now all you have to do is start posting—slowly, at your own pace. Remember, a little is better than nothing. You've got this!

Key points for building your personal brand

Whether you're managing your brand or just starting out, it's an ongoing process. Here are some key points to help you manage/start (and even enjoy) building your brand:

Take time to build your brand
Building a brand doesn't happen overnight. It requires effort and patience. Dedicate time to developing your brand strategy, understanding your audience, and refining your message. Invest in creating high-quality content from time to time, engaging with your audience regularly. The effort you put into building your brand will pay off in the long run.

Consistency is key

One of the most important rules in brand management is consistency. This means that your messages, tone, and visual identity should remain uniform across all platforms and communications. Whether you're posting on social media, writing a blog, or giving a presentation, your brand should always be instantly recognizable and coherent.

Awareness of how you are perceived

It's crucial to maintain an awareness of how you present yourself and how you're perceived by others. This includes both your online and your offline presence. Regularly evaluate your communications and interactions to ensure they align with your brand values and goals. By being mindful of your expression and presentation, you will naturally feel the urge to manage it better. This self-awareness leads to improved brand consistency and a stronger overall image.

Leveraging tools for efficiency

There are countless tools available to help you build and maintain your brand efficiently. From AI content/text tools to social media management platforms to design platforms and many others, learn about these and use them to leverage your brand in the best way possible.

Think of building your brand as an invitation to express your beauty to the world. It's an opportunity to share your unique story, values, and vision. Embrace this opportunity to connect with your stakeholders or target audience on a deeper level and show them what makes you and your business or work so special.

A rainy revelation about branding on Wall Street

It was one of those rainy winter days in New York, where the rain seemed determined to soak you through no matter how fast you moved. I rushed through the downpour to a meeting on Wall Street with an investor I'd been introduced to, hoping he could offer some valuable advice and maybe even assist the company I'd just joined.

I arrived at the 51st floor and sat across from him in this massive conference room, just the two of us, with the Statue of Liberty just visible through the window. I pitched our startup solution with all the passion I could muster. He stayed silent for what felt like forever before finally speaking.

'Can I be direct?' he asked.

'Absolutely,' I replied, steeling myself.

'Your startup seems like fiction to me,' he said.

Boom! In my mind, I saw every single one of our company's achievements flash before my eyes—our successes, the accolades, the satisfied clients. What was he talking about? But then it struck me: If he'd taken the time to meet with me and say this, there had to be a massive lesson here. No way was I going to let it slip by.

'I really want to know what you mean,' I said, leaning in.

He didn't mince words. His analysts had dug into our company and found tons of inconsistencies in our personal and publicly available information. Our web presence, the founders' profiles, our marketing materials—they were all out of sync. The very information that should have been building our reputation and helping us get funded was a mess. This inconsistency made our brand unreliable. And why would any investor want to recommend, work with, or invest in a company that didn't come across as trustworthy?

That meeting was a game-changer for me.

Clients, recruiters, and investors might not see your potential if your brand isn't solid. Most won't bother explaining why they said no or what you could do to improve your credibility. Your personal brand can make or break your company's chances of getting into the deal flow.

Your personal brand is everywhere—on social networks, on Google, and in what people say about you. That's why it's so important to be aware of it and manage it properly. It's crucial for the success of both your business and your career. If you don't actively manage your brand, you're missing out on creating a competitive advantage. In the process, you're potentially sabotaging your success. Let yourself shine!

Since we're talking about branding and getting to know each other more, let's connect!

You can find me on many social media channels as @Lirone Glikman, such as LinkedIn, Instagram, X (Twitter), Facebook, YouTube and TikTok.

Visit my website to download the workbook for *The Super Connector's Playbook*, to excel in your networking and take your professional and personal life to the next level. Visit: www.lironeglikman.com/TSCPworkbook

Scan me

The bottom line

In this chapter, you learned crucial tools that can make or break your success—how to build your magnetizing personal brand.

We have now determined our goals and identified who can help us reach them. We have done the strategy part of networking and prepared for connecting with people. We have crafted our brand and learned how to share it authentically with the world.

Now we're ready to dive in and establish relationships in a way that allows us to connect more authentically and meaningfully with others. Ready?

6

CONNECT TO ENDLESS OPPORTUNITIES

Communicate with your heart

'I've learned that people will forget what you said, people will forget what you did, but people will never forget how you made them feel.'

— MAYA ANGELOU

R eady to be able to connect with anyone, and open your life to endless opportunities? By the end of this chapter, you'll grasp the formula for doing so.

1. **Let's break the ice!**
2. **The ultimate small talk formula for sparking connections**
3. **The unwritten 'don't talk about' rules**
4. **Human buttons to connect with others**
5. **Put yourself in their shoes**

Connecting with people is simple; it's *so* simple, but people don't do it. It may be the social fears or the misleading scenarios in our heads that keep us away from the great conversations and opportunities that are waiting for each and every one of us— on the other side of 'breaking the ice' with a stranger.

The techniques I'm about to share with you to build meaningful connections are very simple. When you open your heart to strangers, you'll find out how much power you have in you:

- You will influence
- You will connect
- You will enjoy
- You will succeed.

Ready to learn the methods to connect with almost anyone?

It's important to know that connecting with others actually has a biological basis; we, as humans, are wired to release hormones when communicating with others. Different hormones are involved in different types of interactions, and knowing how to activate the release of these hormones for yourself and the other person helps deepen connections and bonds. I'm going to share a simple yet mind-blowing guide on how to activate friendship and trust hormones in others to build stronger connections.

Just promise you will use this information to do good and support others and yourself.

Here are the top hormones that help humanity thrive:

Oxytocin: The 'love hormone' fosters mutual liking, trust, and friendship.
Activate it: Hug, hold hands, spend quality time, show kindness.

Dopamine: Associated with pleasure and motivation to achieve.
Activate it: Achieve goals, try new things, enjoy positive interactions.

Serotonin: Regulates mood and well-being.
Activate it: Sunlight, exercise, healthy diet, social support.

Endorphins: Natural painkillers and euphoria.
Activate it: Exercise, laughter, acts of kindness.

THE SUPER CONNECTOR'S PLAYBOOK

Cortisol: The 'stress hormone' that negatively impacts connection.

Manage it: Reduce stress with mindfulness, sleep, healthy habits, and social support.

Understanding and applying the actions that activate these hormonal influences can help us better connect with people around us and deepen our relationships.

Let's break the ice!

We've all experienced a hesitation to connect with others due to fears, social norms, or the fear of rejection. But guess what? The other person feels the same way, whether they are extroverted or introverted. Breaking the ice is that initial interaction with a stranger or acquaintance, paving the way for further connection and conversation. It's about initiating that first interaction to ignite the connection. Now that we understand what breaking the ice is and how it can help us, here are some engaging ways to do it, including opening lines suitable for various social situations, whether at work, at a conference, or elsewhere. Early on, I developed two ways of addressing ice-breaking – 'the Interactive approach' and 'the Attractive approach'.

While I'm about to share these techniques, remember to adapt them to suit your style:

Interactive approach: Initiating the conversation

- **The Smile tactic** – Look at someone for a bit more than a moment and smile genuinely. This will likely prompt a smile back at you or a greeting; you can introduce yourself from there.

- **The Direct tactic** – *'Hi, I'm [Name], nice to meet you!'* This will be straightforward and help break the ice.

- **The 'Ask' tactic** – *'Excuse me, could you help me with [directions/clarifications/items you need?] By the way, I'm [Name].'* This is a subtle way to start a conversation.

- **The Compliment tactic** – *'I love your [item]. By the way, I'm [Name]. What's your name?'* Compliments, when specific and positive, always spark connections.

- **The Hero tactic** – Whether it's helping someone in need at the office or offering a hand in a busy supermarket queue, starting a conversation from a helpful gesture can lead to meaningful interactions.

The Hero tactic in action

I was at a conference hall at the David Intercontinental Hotel in Tel Aviv, on the phone with a colleague I was supposed to meet, walking back and forth from one end to another, trying to find him. A woman whom I didn't know stared at me all along, realizing I was lost. She decided to approach me and say, 'Hi, nice to meet you, I'm Ofir Ben-Nun Steinberg, you seem like you're looking for something. Can I help?' I said, 'Thank you, yes. I'm supposed to meet a colleague here at the entrance to the Chicago Stock Exchange conference.'

She started to laugh and said, 'Dear, this is the London Stock Exchange conference; the one you need is at the Dan Hotel, you came to the wrong hotel!' Feeling stupid yet relieved, I was grateful for her help. We started talking and soon discovered that we both have fathers who are pilots and mutual friends from Australia. We have similar passions and we bonded right away. It was so clear that this was the beginning of a beautiful life-long friendship, and so it has been. Not only that, but this woman is an inspiring individual I learn so much from, who was the youngest licensed trader on the Israeli Stock Exchange and the first woman to establish a regulated investment house. I'm grateful she helped me that day, so I could enrich my life and hers by having her as a friend.

Attractive approach: Drawing people to you

How do you magnetize people to you? This method is usually best in conferences and other business settings:

- **Attract attention with a standout item** – For example, a shirt with the title 'We are hiring!' Startups do it a lot.

Have a colorful jacket that stands out. My friend, international motivational speaker, author, and entrepreneur Nozer Buchia, used to walk around at conferences holding his book *Why Entrepreneurs Really Fail* with his picture on the cover; it attracted questions from others and got them to engage with him.

- **Have a giveaway** – It might be a special business card (like cards with heat buttons to assess your mood), or any useful item. One time I was given a pen at a surrogacy event; the top part was filled with water and had one little egg and many sperms floating in it. As you can imagine, it started many conversations.

- **Be on stage** – This way, you can invite people to approach you right after you finish your talk.

- **The Q&A hack** – Turning this part into a way for others to get to know you is one of my best networking 'Attractive' tactics. I can best explain it with an anecdote:

The Q&A hack in action

I received an invitation to an event in Berlin hosted by Techstars Accelerator, aimed at local startups, which are my potential clients. The catch? I had no access to the attendees list besides the speakers' names. But that wouldn't stop me. Determined to make the most of it, I connected with the speakers on LinkedIn, asking to have a chat at the event. But how could I ensure I met the right startup founders who could be my potential clients, without even knowing who would attend the conference?

I decided to rely on one of my top tactics: 'The Q&A session move'. Before the panel started, I chose a strategic seat in the second row where I could be easily seen. I patiently waited for the Q&A portion to begin. As the audience started asking questions, most said, 'My question is...' or 'I would like to ask...' But when I was called to pose my question, I said, 'Hi, I'm Lirone. I'm a mentor at Techstars in Tel Aviv, specializing in business development, and my question is...' I then asked a very relevant question that not only contributed to the discussion but also showcased my expertise.

When the session ended, the magic happened (as it always does)—the room responded positively to my introduction, and within minutes, five entrepreneurs approached me with keen interest. 'You do business development?', 'You are a mentor?' they inquired.

As I walked around in the networking part, other startup founders recognized me, and conversations flowed effortlessly. By the end of the event, I had generated several leads and even secured a new client. The lesson here is clear: Finding a way to elegantly introduce yourself publicly can get others to be drawn to you and drive opportunities!

To conclude, I have to say that among these methods for breaking the ice with strangers, my preference is for the simplest, most genuine way: 'Hi, nice to meet you. My name is Lirone, what's yours?' That's when the small talk kicks off.

The ultimate small talk formula for sparking connections

I want to bust a common myth, one that I used to believe in and many others still do. When I was young, I always waited for people to start a conversation with me. I wanted them to show me they liked me before I approached them. But then I learned a staggering truth: When we first meet someone, our brain is trying to gauge if they are friend or foe. Before the other person even starts to talk, our brain does a quick calculation based on a person's look, facial expression, hand gestures, how fast they walk, the tone of their voice, and so on. The power is in realizing that in conversations with new people, you want to signal 'friend' right off the bat, as first impressions are made in seconds.

One day I decided to simply change the way I was used to communicating with people. What if I were the first to approach other people, break the ice with them, and show that I like them and make them feel safe with me? Surely, I would increase my chances to connect with them. I have been doing it ever since because it works like magic! It's so powerful to initiate the conversation and be the one who approaches others.

The rule here is 'Like Others First'. Wear your real smile, use approachable words, and make others feel good next to you.

It's the first step to building good rapport and starting small talk.

What is 'small talk'?

It's the first conversation that 'softens' the communication before going to the 'hard' topics and diving into knowing one another or starting an interview or business discussion. It should set the scene, create a good environment, and also help us assess if we like the other person and wish to continue speaking with them.

If you wish to connect with others, small talk can be a way to access the *'Know-Like-Trust' formula*. It comes from the marketing world and holds that when people like us a bit, know us a bit, and trust us a bit, they are willing to talk to us, possibly help us, buy from us, and build a connection with us. That's what small talk enables us to do!

Also, according to psychologist Robert Cialdini's principles of influence, good and engaging small talk can increase likeability, which in turn increases support, sales, or desired results by up to 200%. Now all you have to do is understand how to conduct good, connecting small talk.

Lirone Glikman's small talk formula

This simple formula will make any conversation fun and engaging. It works well for video, phone, or face-to-face interactions.

I designed this methodology based on research from countless small talk sessions I have conducted around the world. It taps into psychological and social aspects. Conversations like this can take place in five minutes or last an hour, your choice.

The Small Talk Formula – by Lirone Glikman

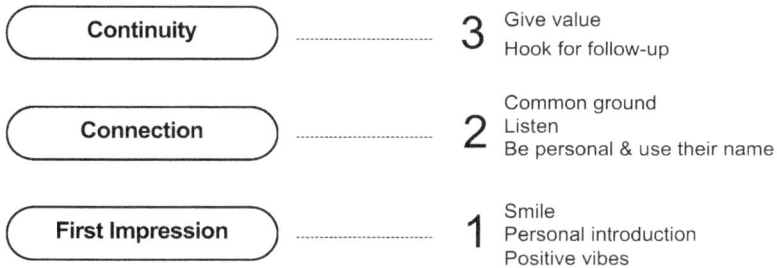

Continuity	....	**3**	Give value Hook for follow-up
Connection	....	**2**	Common ground Listen Be personal & use their name
First Impression	....	**1**	Smile Personal introduction Positive vibes

Small talk Part I – First impression

We form our impression of others within 7–30 seconds. Make sure you start any small talk with:

1. **A smile** – Our non-verbal cues make up 93% of our communication, so smile to give others a sense of safety and indicate that you have good intentions.

2. **Positive topics** – People tend to complain and talk about negative topics when they meet new people or are with those they know. This creates the wrong vibe and builds a new relationship on somewhat negative ground. You want to elevate the vibe and shine bright in any room (or virtual room) you enter. Always find elevating topics: the weather,

your sweet kid, something exciting; compliment others. It's crucial to start with this.

3. **Introduction** – Introduce yourself briefly, ensuring you point out the relevant experience and credentials that will appeal to the person you are speaking with.

The introduction should be tailored to the person you are meeting to make sure you emphasize the right information. I like to follow this basic formula:

- **Past sentence** – What led you here (relevant to the circumstances, e.g., business conference or a friend's dinner).
- **Present sentence** – What you are doing today (should be relevant to the context).
- **Future sentence** – Your goals and aspirations in your current professional or personal circumstances.

An example

Let's say I have a business as a startup consultant. I meet an investor that can potentially get me to work with his portfolio startups; here are some sentences I could use during my introduction that build my credibility and skills in his eyes:

Past: 'I started as an entrepreneur, founding and scaling my own tech venture.'

Present: 'Now, as a startup consultant, I guide emerging startups towards global growth with my strategic expertise.'

Future: 'I'm eager to collaborate with investors and startups to support their growth.'

AI TIP

Use AI text tools to help you craft personalized introductions for different people:

1. Write about your professional background strengths and professional goals.
2. Write your current verbal introduction.
3. Ask it to suggest different introductions based on the above information and tailored to the specific people you're speaking with (e.g. you may introduce yourself differently to an HR person, an investor, and your neighbor whose wife works for the company you just applied for).

Small Talk Part II – Connection

Right after the first impression part, which can last a few minutes, you start the body of the small talk. Your aim is to inject small connecting gestures and strive to create more ties with the person you're talking to.

Doing these three actions repeatedly will help:

1. **State their name/acknowledge them:** You should say their name at least twice, at the beginning and end of the

conversation. Why? Because it is the 'sweetest sound to our ears', as Dale Carnegie said, and it makes people feel heard and acknowledged. If you don't remember their name, it's OK to ask, 'What is your name again?' and repeat it. That will show them you are interested in connecting with them. Also reinforce their points when you agree with them.

2. **Find common ground (my favorite):** This is by far the STRONGEST way to connect with people, and here's why: Common ground makes us feel safe. It is a primal trait from our ancestors in tribal days. When someone met another person who shared common ground, such as clothing, signs, or language, they felt safe knowing they were from the same tribe. If there was no common ground, they felt in danger. You know how when you talk to someone and discover common ground—like having mutual friends or studying at the same university or loving the same band—you feel a bit closer to them? That's what I want you to do several times during the small talk.

How do you do it? Talk about these topics, using my **'4Ps formula for common ground'**:

Passions | Places | People | Present

*   **Passions:** Passions always light up the energy in the room. You know how we all enjoy talking about what we love (sports, trips, hobbies, kids, etc.). Make sure to ask them about the things they love.

- **Places:** Talk about places you share: places you've traveled to or love, cities you grew up in or have been to or worked at, museums, universities, and so on.

- **People:** Discuss people you have in common and both like, from mutual friends to celebrities to lecturers. It always connects and builds trust and closeness.

- **Present:** This one refers to what we share right now, together, like the weather, commenting on each other's clothes, smells, the event we are attending, the wallpaper, the reality show we all like to watch. Talk about things happening in your sphere now—as long as you keep the conversation positive.

The 4Ps of Common Ground – by Lirone Glikman

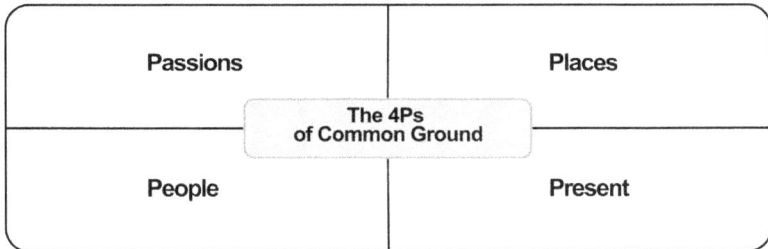

Passions	Places
	The 4Ps of Common Ground	
People	Present

3. **Listen with curiosity:** This one has two sides—one is about listening, and the second is about asking questions to get them to share more about themselves. First, harness your curiosity and find interest in them. This is mainly non-verbal, although you can say, 'Yes, I hear you', 'Wow',

'Amazing'. If you nod your head, you are signaling that you are acknowledging them. It is said that if you nod your head at least three times, the other person may speak 30% more. The questions you can ask to show interest are the reporter's questions (who, what, why, where, how), open-ended so people will get to share more about themselves. For example:

- Why do you do what you do?
- What is the most exciting project you are currently working on?
- What was the most exciting part of this event so far?
- What brought you here?
- How can I help you?
- Can you share advice on…?
- How did you overcome [challenge they mentioned]?
- What are your thoughts on [topic they mentioned]?
- Can you elaborate on [point they mentioned]?
- What led you to pursue [interest they mentioned]?
- Can you share a bit more about [experience they mentioned]?
- What has been the highlight of your [recent experience they mentioned]?

Small Talk Part III – Continuity

At the end of a conversation or meeting, you should decide if you want to continue cultivating a relationship with this person. If you are seeking a job and this person can help you find one, you would want to keep in touch. If this person has a simi-lar business to yours, you may not be so keen to stay in touch, as you may not be able to immediately help each other. On the other hand, if you had a great time speaking with them, you may want to keep in touch. If you decide you want to continue the discussion, exchange contact information and make sure to do two things: share a *value* that the other person can benefit from, and include a *hook*.

Value

What value can you offer? Remember, we said the true cur-rency of networking is giving and helping others—without keeping score. Be the first to give.

So what can you give? Anything that you recognize the other person may need:

- Give advice about a burning issue they share or that occurs in their industry.
- Send them an article about a topic you talked about that interests them.
- Share your CV or someone else's who is looking for a job.
- Offer to provide feedback on their projects or ideas.
- Share relevant industry insights or market trends.
- Introduce them to valuable contacts in your network.
- Provide access to exclusive events or webinars.
- Share useful tools or resources that can benefit their work.
- Offer to mentor or provide guidance based on your expertise.

- Provide support or assistance with their personal or professional goals.
- And many more.

Hook

Make sure to tell them you will be in touch, so they actually expect to hear from you in one or two days. Thus, when you call them or send that CV, it won't be weird—they were waiting to hear from you. Then you continue following up (more on that in the next chapter) and building your relationships in your business.

The small talk formula arranges all those communication activities in a coherent way and helps us to build the small talk towards connecting and future engagement. And the best part? It works for everyone.

The unwritten 'don't talk about' rules

When engaging in professional conversations with someone for the first time, or when talking to someone from a culture different from yours, it's crucial to navigate topics with sensitivity and tact. Here are some key areas to avoid getting into to maintain positive and productive interactions. (After engaging with them for a while, you might feel more comfortable talking about these topics and other personal ones.)

Avoid these topics

- **Don't say you'll be in touch if you won't:** This one is more a behavior than a subject. It's essential to be genuine and honest in your interactions. If you promise to follow up or stay in touch, make sure you intend to do so. Empty promises can damage your credibility and undermine trust in your professional relationships.

- **Politics:** Political discussions can be divisive and may lead to disagreements or tension, particularly in professional settings. It's best to avoid delving into political topics unless you are certain it is appropriate and welcomed by all parties involved.

- **Salary:** Discussing salary can be sensitive and may lead to discomfort, especially if there are disparities or differences in compensation among individuals. It's generally not advisable to bring up salary-related matters unless it is explicitly relevant to the conversation or context.

- **Any topic that can 'break you apart':** This refers to sensitive or contentious subjects that have the potential to create conflict or cause offense. Possible examples include religion, personal beliefs, or controversial social issues. It's important to exercise discretion and avoid discussing topics that could disrupt the harmony of the conversation or relationship. Instead, focus on topics that foster mutual understanding, respect, and collaboration.

Be sensitive, but also be brave enough to push the boundaries at the right pace when needed. Essentially, as you open up and talk about more personal topics, you get closer and closer. It may take an hour or a year, so be sensitive as you consciously deepen your relationship.

Human buttons to connect with others

In the intricate dance of human interaction, there are some fundamental 'buttons' as I like to call them, that, when pressed, facilitate seamless connection and rapport, often transcending any cultural differences. Understanding and leveraging these psychological triggers can enrich our social interactions and deepen our relationships. Here are five human buttons to help us navigate the intricate maze of human connection.

- **We connect to happy people**
  The contagious nature of positivity is a powerful force in social dynamics. When we encounter individuals who exude joy and enthusiasm, it sparks a resonance within us. A simple smile can light up a room and pave the way for meaningful interaction. By embodying positivity and radiating enthusiasm, we create an inviting atmosphere that magnetizes others towards us.

- **We all like to talk about ourselves**
  One of the most effective ways to establish rapport is by showing genuine interest in others. People love to share

their experiences, thoughts, and aspirations. By becoming a skilled listener and actively engaging in conversations, we signal that we value and respect their perspective. Listening attentively and asking thoughtful questions not only fosters connection but also allows us to gain insights into their world.

- **We connect to familiarity**
  Finding common ground connects individuals, transcending differences and fostering a sense of camaraderie. Whether it's shared interests, experiences, or values, identifying commonalities creates a sense of belonging and mutual understanding (e.g., using my '4Ps formula for common ground'). By actively seeking out common ground, we lay the foundation for meaningful connections that transcend surface-level interactions.

- **We like to feel special**
  Personalization adds a touch of warmth and sincerity to our interactions, making others feel valued and appreciated. Taking the time to tailor our communication to the individual demonstrates attentiveness and thoughtfulness. Whether it's remembering a personal detail or acknowledging their achievements, personalized gestures create a lasting impression and deepen the bond between individuals.

- **We give back when we receive**
  Reciprocity forms the cornerstone of social exchange, where acts of kindness and generosity are met with reciprocal gestures. By adding value to our interactions, whether through sharing knowledge, offering assistance, or providing support, we create a positive cycle of giving and receiving. By contributing to the well-being of others, we cultivate a network of goodwill and strengthen our social connections.

In essence, understanding these human buttons empowers us to navigate social interactions with finesse and authenticity. By incorporating these principles into our communication repertoire, we can forge deeper connections, nurture meaningful relationships, and enrich our lives with the tapestry of human connection. That may also lead to achieving desired results for both us and them.

Put yourself in their shoes

Connecting with others is a delicate dance of understanding what they value and finding ways to offer something meaningful in return while being faithful to yourself and your boundaries. Zig Ziglar's timeless advice rings true: *'If you help enough people get what they want, you'll get what you want.'*

So, what do they want? Whether it's the CEO of a company, an HR manager, your direct boss, or even your neighbor, each individual has unique needs and desires. The key is to identify these needs and consider what you can offer in return—and stand out by doing so.

For the CEO of a company, it might be a fresh perspective, innovative ideas, or valuable insights that can propel their business forward. Similarly, for an HR manager, connecting them with other qualified candidates or offering assistance in their recruitment efforts (especially if you are being interviewed by them) can strengthen your relationship in some way, and establish you as a reliable resource they want as a part of their company.

When it comes to your direct boss, offering support, providing solutions to challenges they face, or simply lending a listening ear can go a long way in building trust and rapport. Finally, even interactions with your neighbor can be enriched by small gestures, like offering to collect their mail or giving them a genuine compliment. By understanding what others need and finding ways to meet those needs, you not only strengthen your connections and stand out, but also create a network of goodwill that can benefit you in return.

To become more adept at connecting with others and understanding their needs, it's crucial to take proactive steps. Cultivate a mindset of generosity and reciprocity, knowing that by helping others achieve their goals, you pave the way for mutual success.

EXERCISE

Practice the small talk formula.

Apply this formula at an upcoming business meeting, industry event, or meetup. Go over it and plan in advance how to navigate all its phases in the right way for you.

Visit my website to download the workbook for *The Super Connector's Playbook*, to excel in your networking and take your professional and personal life to the next level. Visit: www.lironeglikman.com/TSCPworkbook

The bottom line

Make sure to think about how it can work for you—for your culture, work environment, character, abilities, circumstances. Experiment, connect, and try different approaches until it feels right. Always remember:

- Be proactive! Be the first to introduce yourself.
- Be curious to know about others and ask questions.
- Be open with others and share info about yourself.

Now practice it.

If you've established new strong connections, that's fantastic! But remember, maintaining them is the real key. Without staying in touch, your efforts may lose their value over time.

In the next chapter, we'll explore strategies for effective communication and relationship maintenance.

7

THE 'WORKING' PART OF NETWORKING

Nurturing meaningful connections— strengthen those relationships

'The richest people in the world look for and build networks, everyone else looks for work.'

— ROBERT KIYOSAKI

We meet so many people in life. If you don't keep in touch with relevant ones, it's like a waste of your time, and it blocks so many opportunities from coming into your professional and personal life. It can be challenging to hold on to relationships, but I have prepared some great techniques for you.

In this chapter you will learn:

1. **The power of maintaining relationships**
2. **Why maintaining relationships is challenging for most**
3. **Your prosperity circle of contacts**
4. **How to maintain relationships**
5. **Trust-building**
6. **What if they don't respond to you?**

The power of maintaining relationships

Why maintain relationships? To enjoy the human experience to the max! To feel belonging by being surrounded by different people, to be able to help them and also fulfill yourself through them.

It can be seen as tedious to maintain relationships with people who are not close to you, but it provides us with emotional, career and job security and access to fulfillment the same as we provide to them. When you build those relationships over time, this is where the magic happens.

What is the power of building relationships?

- **Support and connection:** Relationships provide emotional support, companionship, and a sense of belonging, which are vital for mental and emotional well-being.

- **Networking and opportunities:** Maintaining relationships opens doors to new opportunities in both personal and professional life, leading to jobs, collaborations, and friendships.

- **Personal growth:** Interacting with others promotes personal growth by exposing you to different perspectives, cultures, and ways of thinking, which can broaden your horizons and deepen your understanding of the business world.

- **Mutual benefit:** Healthy relationships are based on reciprocity, with both parties contributing and benefiting. This mutual support includes offering and receiving encouragement, assistance, and support when needed.

- **Happiness and fulfillment:** Positive relationships enhance overall happiness and fulfillment, providing life satisfaction and a sense of purpose and meaning.

Relationships are built by multiple touch points, by experiences shared and diverse interactions—online and in person, over time. That's how we get to know others and build trust.

Sounds overwhelming? It really isn't. Here's how to do it!

Why maintaining relationships is challenging for most

Many people avoid maintaining relationships and following up because they believe they're not good at it. They hesitate to reach out, fearing they might intrude on others. They also find continuous communication tedious and doubt why anyone they barely know would want to help them. This reluctance often comes from social fears and a lack of confidence in their own worthiness of attention.

The funny thing is that they've got it all wrong—for example, when, with my encouragement, students do reach out to the people they've targeted, they are usually surprised that the others are happy to hear from them and even support them! It's essential to recognize these internal barriers to understand why we struggle with following up and maintaining relationships. We often realize the mistake of not maintaining relationships when we need something, and by then, it may be too late. It makes us very uncomfortable to approach someone we haven't been in touch with for ages to ask for something.

To 'call people only when we need them' feels wrong and it definitely doesn't work so well in some cases. Therefore, remember the rule: It's always better to build genuine relationships with people long before you may need their help.

Your prosperity circle of contacts

Let's face it, we can't maintain relationships with everyone we ever met, and quite honestly, we don't need to. Throughout our lives, we encounter a variety of people—close family members, friends, and business-related contacts. Effectively managing these relevant connections is crucial for personal and professional growth.

Here's a guide to managing the myriad of people in your network and making sense of it:

Step 1: Categorize your connections
Start by categorizing your contacts into different prosperity circles. Once you have this segmentation in place, you'll be able to identify which circle each new person belongs to and decide how to maintain the relationship. Some connections may require regular interaction, while others might only need to be approached once a year, for example. Here is a suggested way to categorize them:

- **Close relationships:** These are your family, best friends, and closest confidants. They are the people you can rely on and who play a significant role in your life.
- **Loose connections:** These include acquaintances and people you interact with occasionally. They might not be part of your daily life, but they can still offer valuable insights or opportunities.
- **Strategic connections:** These are business-related contacts who can help you advance in your career or business. They might include mentors, industry leaders, and potential clients or partners.

Step 2: Identify your top 30 contacts

Next, create a list of 10–30 most important people you need to meet and get to know better these days. (You can update this list periodically based on your needs.) This 'lobby' should include individuals who can have a significant impact on your personal or professional life. Write down their names and prioritize getting to know them better.

Step 3: Use a personal CRM system

To keep track of your network, create a list using Excel sheets, or any personal CRM (Customer Relationship Management) system that works for you. Add the 30 people you identified earlier and regularly update this list. Include relevant details such as how you met, the last time you interacted, topics you have discussed, and any follow-up actions needed. Managing a large network can be challenging, but using the right tools can make it easier. Personal CRM systems help you organize your contacts, schedule follow-ups, and maintain consistent communication.

As mentioned earlier, studies suggest that the human brain can remember up to 150 individuals. While it's not feasible to remember or maintain relationships with everyone you know, using a listing or CRM tool can help you manage your network effectively.

Step 4: Regularly evaluate and update your network

Finally, regularly evaluate and update your list. People's importance and relevance to your goals can change over time. Periodically review your list, categorize new contacts, and update your information to ensure you stay on top of your relationships and can capitalize on opportunities as they arise.

By categorizing your contacts, focusing on your top 30, using a personal CRM, and regularly updating your network, you can build and maintain a robust and effective prosperity circle of relevant contacts to keep close. This can potentially open up new opportunities for success.

How to maintain relationships

I have said that maintaining relationships is the 'working' part of the word 'networking'. This is because once you know your network and whom you want to keep building your relationship with, it becomes a question of actually doing it. This is where so many people quit (or don't even start), because they don't know how to proceed. But fear not: When it comes to maintaining relationships, it's all about *Communication* and *System*. Here is how you can do it.

1. Communication

To maintain and build relationships, you should communicate consistently in a way that is both elegant and genuine. But how? It involves what I call 'drops of presence'.

You can give your drops of presence in two ways:

- **Care communication:** This involves showing genuine direct interest in someone by asking about their well-being, family, or projects, or engaging with topics they've discussed before. It also includes offering help or sending relevant articles. Building on these interactions, you can suggest continuing the conversation through a phone call, setting up a meeting, or simply leaving it at 'touching base'.

- **Visibility communication:** This refers to simply being present and engaging with others on a high level, ensuring that you are remembered and recognized. This can be achieved through likes or comments online, or participating in group discussions on social media platforms, saying hello in the hallway, or seeing them at industry events or around the neighborhood.

'Drops of Presence' Communication for Maintaining Relationships

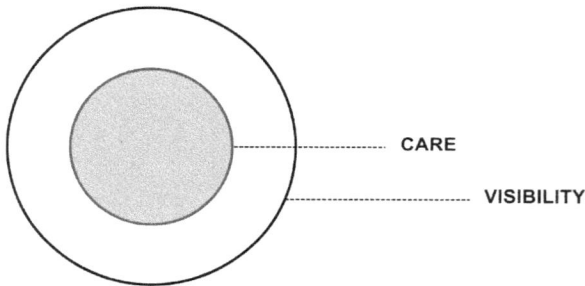

CARE

VISIBILITY

2. System

Apply communication within a system. There are various methods and tools to systematize relationship maintenance that go beyond the familiar tactics of sending holiday greetings or birthday wishes, which I highly recommend. My general network hears from me at least twice a year: at New Year's and on another big occasion. I spend time crafting a greeting and sending it via email and WhatsApp, as well as posting on social media.

Two other primary systems include *Association* and the *90-List Method*.

- **Association:** It's an intuitive one—when someone or something reminds you of a specific individual, you send them a message. For instance, if you pass by a Nike store and remember a colleague/friend who loves Nike, you might send them a message saying, 'I thought of you when I passed by Nike today, how are you?' If you find yourself chatting with another coworker about a *third* teammate, you might text them to say, 'Hi, [name], I was just talking about you with [teammate's name], so I wanted to say hi.' We all enjoy knowing others are caring about us, and this is a nice touch base to acknowledge them and nothing more, but it can potentially lead to more down the line.

- **90-List Method:** This structured approach by marketer Michael Port involves identifying key decision-makers and important individuals (personally or professionally) whom you want to build relationships with. There should be no more than 90 people on the list (which can include the list of your top 30 contacts I previously asked you to create). You then dedicate around ten minutes each day to communicating with up to three of these key contacts through the 'drops of presence' tactic above (*care* or *visibility* messages). Within a month, you will touch base once with each person on your list.

Repeat the process each month, and you can update the list as needed to reflect changes in your network or priorities. This ensures regular contact with all significant connections over the course of a month to keep you in their memories until the day you may wish to contact them for business reasons. Assign a specific ten-minute slot in your daily calendar for this activity, and you'll be on your way to managing your network like a professional!

It's worth repeating: It's always better to build genuine relationships with people long before you may need their help!

Trust-building

Cultivating trust and building connections takes time and effort, but strong relationships are invaluable when you are seeking support or assistance. By investing in genuine connections and demonstrating reliability, empathy, and generosity, you lay the foundation for meaningful relationships built on trust and mutual support. Here's what you can do.

- **Establish genuine connections:** Take the time to genuinely connect with others, whether it's through shared interests, experiences, or values. Authentic relationships foster trust and are more likely to yield positive responses when you are asking for help.

- **Be reliable and consistent:** Demonstrate reliability and consistency in your interactions with others. Follow through on commitments and be dependable. Consistency builds trust and reliability, making others more willing to assist you when needed.

- **Show empathy and understanding:** Demonstrate empathy and understanding toward others' perspectives and situations. Actively listening and showing empathy fosters deeper connections and builds trust. People are more inclined to help those they feel understand and care about them.

- **Offer assistance without expecting anything in return:** Be proactive in offering assistance and support to others without expecting reciprocation. Acts of kindness and generosity create goodwill and strengthen relationships. When you are in need, people are more likely to reciprocate the help you've offered.

These are important building blocks for any relationship, and they will ensure a strong one over years to come.

What if they don't respond to you?

It happens to everyone—you reach out to a colleague or professional contact, and you get no response. Being 'ghosted' can be frustrating, but it's important not to take it personally. People have various reasons for not responding promptly, such as simply being busy or distracted by other issues. Here's a way to handle this phenomenon and maintain professionalism.

Types of follow-up emails you can send

1. Initial follow-up email
2. Engaging with valuable insights email

AI TIP

Leverage AI text tools to craft your emails effectively. Here are some tips to prompt it well:

- Personalization: Share the person's professional background, their relevant information, and the essence of your email, so the AI can personalize your emails.
- Subject line optimization: Use AI to generate multiple subject lines and choose the one you think will have the highest predicted open rate.
- Tone and clarity: Use AI to ensure your emails are clear, concise, and professional, optimizing the tone to be close to your voice, remaining friendly yet assertive.

Email scripts

(Remember to adapt these to your needs and circumstances.)

1. **Initial follow-up email:** If you don't get a response to your initial email, it's okay to follow up twice or more. Here is a sample follow-up email.

Hi [Colleague's Name],
I hope this message finds you well. I wanted to follow up on my previous email regarding [briefly mention the topic]. I understand you have a busy schedule and might have missed it.
Whenever you get a chance, I'd appreciate your thoughts on this.
Thank you for your time and consideration.

Best regards,
[Your Name]

2. **Engaging with valuable insights email:** If there's still no response, try sending an email with valuable data or resources that might interest them. This shows you're not just reaching out for your benefit but offering something useful to them. Here's a sample email.

Hi [Colleague's Name],
I came across this article/data/report on [briefly mention the topic] and thought you might find it interesting given your work in [mention their field or project].

I'd still be happy to get on a call to discuss [original topic] whenever you have time. Please let me know what works best for you.

Best regards,
[Your Name]

Focus on responsive relationships

Ultimately, it's important to focus on nurturing relationships with those who are responsive and reciprocate your efforts. Choose the ones you want in your network wisely and respect yourself, just as you respect others. Building a network is about quality, not just quantity; valuing mutual respect and engagement will help you foster stronger, more meaningful professional connections.

Renewed relationships that boosted my business

I met Shai Doitsh and Sharon Jägermann when I was running my event production company at the beginning of my career, and we have kept in touch over the years, exchanging holiday greetings and staying connected through Facebook. I haven't missed the chance to touch base at least once a year with them, considering them a part of my network of people I enjoy working with and personally like. Fast forward about 15 years. I was in Austin, Texas attending a conference when I unexpectedly spotted Shai and Sharon there! It was exciting to see familiar faces of people I love, in such a different setting. We caught up, laughed, and talked about some memories from the old times.

During our conversation, they mentioned working in a European organization called ICE and hinted that they might need someone with my skills as a speaker and events moderator for a few big projects. Later, I sent them several follow-up emails. When they didn't answer, I didn't give up or take it personally. Instead, I sent a personal text message, which eventually helped, and we set up a meeting to start crafting our plan of action together. Eight months later, I found myself collaborating with them on events in Barcelona, Berlin, Madrid, and Vienna, and making an important impact on their organization's communities across Europe. Together, we did great work that I'm so proud of.

It's incredible how that initial bond we formed years ago, along with the effort we put into maintaining our relationship over the years, paid off for both of our missions! Meeting them again served as a reminder of our good connection, making it easy for them to consider me for job opportunities.

EXERCISE

Daily habits.

a. Create a list of 5–10 people whom it is important for you to maintain contact with because they hold professional significance for you.

_____

_____

_____

_____

_____

b. Allocate ten minutes daily in your schedule to reach out to one person each day for the next ten days using the 'drops of presence' tactic (*care* or *visibility* messages).

c. Mark your calendar for the 1st of next month to review the list and repeat the process.

Start small and make it a daily habit—it will become one of your greatest assets.

Visit my website to download the workbook for *The Super Connector's Playbook*, to excel in your networking and take your professional and personal life to the next level. Visit: www.lironeglikman.com/TSCPworkbook

The bottom line

As we cultivate our relationships with our network, maintaining regular communication lays the foundation for potential mutual professional and emotional support. People will like you more and be drawn to you simply because you remembered them and showed that you cared!

It's crucial to establish a system for managing your contacts and relationships. This is not a step to overlook, regardless of your position or the number of people you attract. Maintaining relationships is key to long-term success.

Transitioning from fostering connections to obtaining tangible results raises some questions. Do friends or acquaintances have an obligation to assist us? And how can we effectively leverage these relationships to garner support when required? Let's dive into these queries to uncover strategies for achieving tangible outcomes from our networks.

8

GET THE RESULTS YOU WANT

Help them thrive, and you'll find fulfillment.

*'What you get by achieving your
goals is not as important as what you
become by achieving your goals.'*

— Zig Ziglar

'With so many connections, why aren't you a millionaire yet?' My friend who is a very good networker was once asked. Another well-connected friend said something similar when she was job hunting: 'How come I know so many people and have helped so many, yet I can't find a job?'

This question comes up every now and then—and rightfully so.

NEWSFLASH: We all have a network of connections. Excellent!

I always say that relationships make us rich—they lead to fulfillment, opportunities, success, money, friendships, intimate connections, personal growth, and much more—just as we can offer the same to others. Yet, reaching those goals often takes more than simply having a vast network.

What steps can we take to ensure that our connections effectively help us achieve our goals? And equally important, how can we help the people in our network achieve theirs? It requires a combination of actions and circumstances.

Here's what we'll talk about in this chapter.

1. **Ask smart: Avoid common mistakes**
2. **Know their needs, gain their support**
3. **The classic way to get help**
4. **The power of gratitude**

Ask smart: Avoid common mistakes

The basic truth that so many people are unable to see is that people can help us achieve ANYTHING we want in life. That's because we humans are a community-oriented species. We engage in collaboration and support to survive and thrive!

With that mindset we can potentially ask absolutely anything and expect to get many of our requests fulfilled, at least to some extent. From a professional point of view, you can make various requests of others, depending on your goals and the context of the interaction. Here are some common requests you can make:

- **Advice or guidance:** Seek advice from experienced professionals on career decisions, skill development, or navigating challenges in your field.

- **Learn about others:** Speak to professionals in your field to learn more about their career paths, industries, or specific topics of interest.

- **Referrals or introductions:** Request introductions to other professionals in their network who may be able to provide valuable insights or opportunities.

- **Feedback:** Ask for feedback on your resumé, portfolio, or professional profile to help you improve and present yourself more effectively.

- **Recommendations or endorsements:** Request recommendations or endorsements on platforms like LinkedIn to strengthen your professional reputation.

- **Collaborations or partnerships:** Explore potential collaborations or partnerships with professionals who have complementary skills or shared interests.

- **Job or internship opportunities:** Inquire about job openings or internship positions within their organization or industry network.

- **Industry insights or trends:** Seek insights into current industry trends, challenges, or opportunities that could inform your career decisions or strategies.

- **Networking events or communities:** Ask for invitations to relevant networking events, conferences, or online communities where you can expand your professional network.

And there are many more.

Top mistakes we make when asking

Have friends ever helped you? I'm sure they did. Why did they do it? Because they are your friends. Has a stranger ever helped you? Why? Probably because you sparked something in them and they liked you; it might simply be the fact that you asked for their help in a way that made them feel good. While it never hurts to ask, there are mistakes we can make in the *way* we ask. No one teaches us how to form requests, and it is helpful to deploy the kind of manners that get a person *wanting* to help you.

Once, when I lived in Sydney, I received a voice message from an old colleague from my home country who had the habit of obsessively asking me to connect him with others from my wide network. While I was happy to help him at first, I had had enough when I felt I was being used. I had been out of the country for six months already when he left me this message:

'Why are you abroad?! I need your help ASAP!'

I said to myself, 'Helloooo, I don't work for you. I will help you if you make me want to help you, but with that attitude, it's not likely.' It creates antagonism and makes me want to part ways as opposed to connect further and give help.

So what are some mistakes many of us tend to make when asking for help and how do we fix them?

- **Disrespectful requests:** People who ask too firmly ('You owe me something' attitude, 'Give me this', or 'Do this') are doing it all wrong.

  Fix: We should make people feel good about the chance to help us. You can even say 'Whether you can or can't, I will still respect you and be grateful that you considered trying...'

- **Not being specific:** This is such a common mistake. I have received many requests that are so vague that I wondered if the person really wanted to get that support. An example is asking broad questions like, *'I am searching for a job in marketing. Can you help?'*

  Fix: Be specific with your request. In this case, before making it ask yourself these questions: What type of marketing? Digital marketing or strategy? Campaign? Partnerships? Which industry? What level of role? and so on. The more specific you are, the better others will be able to help you.

- **Requests for general introductions:** When asking a friend for an introduction to a third party, many people simply say, 'Just connect us.' This approach often reduces the chances of a successful connection, because your friend will fail to convey the key message that might motivate the third party to engage.

  Fix: To optimize this process, provide your friend with a brief description of yourself, including why the connection matters. Use a few key points for them to share or an email to forward. Don't leave the introduction entirely to them; highlight your unique qualities or accomplishments that will engage the other person. Help your friend effectively 'sell' you to the third party.

EXERCISE

Reflection.

These communication mistakes can ruin your chances of getting the support you need. As you consider these points, also reflect on how others have asked you for help. What made you want to help them? What didn't?

_____

_____

_____

_____

_____

Know their needs, gain their support

Whenever I find myself around new people, my focus is always on the 'What's in it for them?' (WIIFT) aspect to connect better and also drive results. This mindset proved invaluable during an unexpectedly long stay in Berlin after a canceled flight, with no new flight in sight for several weeks. Determined to make the most of my time, I reached out to friends to expand my network and get introductions to government and tech-related organizations.

I arranged a meeting with the team at ELNET (European Leadership Network) for the DACH countries. After establishing a bond and good rapport, I strategically used the

WIIFT concept. Understanding that their organization might be hesitant to engage with me, I began by offering free resources and potential support.

Based on my research before our meeting, I assumed the company needed connections to startups for their projects. I also read that they worked in Vienna and had stakeholders there. Additionally, I thought they might need moderators and speakers for their European events.

With that in mind, I said:

'There are several ways I can possibly assist you:
I'm well-connected in the startup scene and can provide access to many startup sectors in my home region.
Additionally, I'll be in Vienna soon and would be happy to share my knowledge and support your goals while there.
I offer speaking engagements on topics like global networking, leadership, and personal branding. As a seasoned conference moderator, I can assist with events as well.'

This approach resonated with them, leading to an invitation to speak at a private meeting at the Austrian Parliament with four parliament members, sharing my knowledge about supporting tech collaboration during challenging times. This opportunity not only utilized my expertise but also strengthened our relationship. We stayed in genuine touch over time, and six months later they offered me a paid project, solidifying both our commercial and our friendly relationship. I acted as a co-moderator for a conference about digital health in Berlin, with Prof. Dr. Karl Lauterbach, Germany's Federal Minister of Health at the time among the esteemed attendees.

The 'What's in it for them?' concept is a fundamental aspect of human psychology that revolves around self-interest and motivation. Essentially, it suggests that people are more likely to engage in or support something if they perceive a benefit or gain from doing so. Understanding this concept allows you to empathize with others' perspectives and motivations, ultimately driving mutually beneficial results.

Here's how you can understand 'What's in it for them?'

- **Be in their spot:** Try to empathize with the other person's needs, desires, and concerns. Consider what they value and what might motivate them to take action or support a particular cause.
- **Listen actively:** Pay close attention to what the other person is saying and observe their body language and reactions. This can provide valuable insights into their interests and priorities.
- **Ask questions:** Engage in open and genuine conversations with the other person to better understand their perspective. Ask questions that encourage them to share their thoughts, feelings, and motivations.
- **Highlight benefits:** When presenting your ideas or proposals to others, focus on highlighting the benefits that are

relevant to them. Clearly communicate what they stand to gain by supporting your cause or taking action.

- **Tailor your approach:** Recognize that different people may have different needs, then tailor your approach and messaging to resonate with their specific needs and interests.

By understanding and acknowledging the WIIFT concept in others, you can effectively personalize your communication and actions to appeal to their motivations and interests, ultimately strengthening your connections and relationships.

The classic way to get help

There is one method that can make almost anyone want to help you, whether they're a stranger or a foe: the Ben Franklin Effect.

One of the most compelling examples of the Ben Franklin Effect comes from Benjamin Franklin himself. In his biography, he recounts how he transformed a political adversary into a friend during his time in the Pennsylvania Assembly. Despite facing harsh criticism from a fellow member, Franklin chose not to respond with hostility. Instead, he took a different approach—he asked his adversary for a favor.

Franklin asked to borrow a rare book from the person's personal collection. Surprisingly, the adversary agreed and provided Franklin with the book. Franklin promptly returned it, expressing gratitude for the kindness shown. At the next assembly, the opponent who had previously criticized Franklin greeted him with smiles. Over time, this political enemy became a supporter and close friend of Franklin's.

Why does the Ben Franklin Effect work?

The Ben Franklin Effect capitalizes on a psychological principle known as cognitive dissonance. Cognitive dissonance occurs when our beliefs or behaviors contradict each other, causing mental discomfort. Humans naturally seek internal consistency and strive to resolve conflicting thoughts or actions. When we perform a favor for someone we initially perceived negatively, it creates cognitive dissonance. Our behavior contradicts our negative perception, leading to discomfort. To reduce this dissonance, our mind adjusts our attitudes to align with our actions. In the context of the Ben Franklin Effect, when we ask someone for a favor, they are more likely to comply due to the principle of consistency. Once they have performed the favor, their mind seeks to align their attitudes with their actions, resulting in a shift in perception towards us.

This is actually what I call 'The Oldest Trick in the Book to Get Others to Help Us,' which is asking for advice or a favor. As explained, when you ask for a favor or advice genuinely, the other person convinces themselves that you are a good person and they want you to succeed. As a result, they are more likely to provide valuable advice or even make an effort to help find a solution. This approach has proven effective for various situations, from finding an apartment to reaching clients or getting assistance in sales and projects.

Use it sincerely, and you'll increase your chances of achieving your goals and fulfilling your potential!

The power of gratitude

I have always been a very grateful person; I say thank you for everything. When I was young, this habit originated from my tendency to please others and feeling undeserving, but as I grew older, I realized that genuine gratitude, expressed with sincerity in your eyes, can go a long way. It makes people feel seen and happy that they could help you; it brings you closer together.

Now, let's expand on the importance of saying thanks in human interactions.

The physical aspect: Expressing gratitude has tangible effects on our physical well-being. It is known that when we express gratitude, our bodies release oxytocin, the 'love hormone'. Oxytocin not only promotes feelings of trust and connection as mentioned earlier, but also reduces stress and anxiety. Moreover, the act of expressing gratitude has been linked to improved heart health, lower blood pressure, and better immune function. Thus, saying 'thanks' not only benefits our mental health but also contributes to our overall physical well-being.

The psychological aspect: Gratitude has profound psychological effects on both the giver and the recipient. For the person expressing gratitude, it fosters a sense of positivity and well-being. By acknowledging and appreciating the kindness of others, we cultivate a mindset of abundance, which can lead to greater resilience in the face of challenges. For the recipient, receiving gratitude boosts self-esteem and enhances feelings of competence and worthiness. It reinforces positive behaviors and encourages continued acts of kindness and generosity. Overall, gratitude promotes a healthier and more optimistic outlook on life, contributing to greater psychological resilience and well-being.

The goal achievement aspect: In addition to its physical and psychological benefits, gratitude also plays a crucial role in achieving our goals. When we express gratitude for the support, guidance, or assistance we receive from others, we strengthen our relationships and build social capital. This, in turn, creates a supportive network of individuals willing to lend a helping hand or offer valuable insights and resources. Moreover, expressing gratitude fosters a culture of reciprocity and collaboration, where individuals are more inclined to support one another's goals and aspirations. By cultivating a habit of gratitude in our interactions, we not only nurture positive relationships but also increase our likelihood of success in achieving our goals.

In summary, the power of gratitude in human interaction extends beyond mere politeness—it has profound physical, psychological, and goal achievement implications. By expressing genuine gratitude, we enhance our own well-being, foster positive relationships, and create a supportive environment conducive to personal and collective growth.

EXERCISE

To leverage your network for results, ask yourself:

a. Whom can you help with something important to them?

_____

_____

_____

b. From whom have you failed to seek advice? And what's stopping you from doing so?

_____

_____

_____

Just do it!

Scan me

Visit my website to download the workbook for *The Super Connector's Playbook*, to excel in your networking and take your professional and personal life to the next level. Visit: www.lironeglikman.com/TSCPworkbook

The bottom line

If you want your network to help you achieve your goals, start by helping them achieve theirs. Give genuinely, maintain relationships authentically, and bring your best self to every situation.

The process of building and benefiting from relationships is rarely linear. Connections develop uniquely and at different speeds. Understanding this helps you navigate relationships more effectively. There is an abundance of people you can help, just as they can help you, but recognize that each relationship may follow its own path and timeline.

My *Human Factor* Method also progresses in varied ways and at different paces. By understanding and practicing these principles, you'll know how to build strong connections. People will naturally be drawn to you, and you'll see the results in your life.

9

SUPERCHARGE YOUR CAREER AND LIFE FULFILLMENT

Time to create a fulfilling life through the power of relationships!

*'Go confidently in the direction of your dreams.
Live the life you have imagined.'*

— HENRY DAVID THOREAU

Congratulations! You have made it to the end of the book. By now you have learned the *Human Factor* Method, skills that will help you to fulfill yourself in life through the power of relationship-building. You have learned how to build them authentically and strategically, and how to become a magnet for others who can transform your life, just as you can transform theirs. By now you know that networking is something we are all meant to do.

Here is a recap of the main pillars we have discussed:

1. **Goal setting:** Establishing clear objectives that you want to achieve to fulfill your needs and dreams (Chapter 3).

2. **People planning:** Being strategic about whom to connect with, so they can help you achieve your goals (Chapter 4).

3. **Personal branding:** Crafting and showcasing your unique identity and value proposition to the world, online and offline, in a magnetizing way (Chapter 5).

4. **Connecting:** Actively breaking the ice, connecting and fostering meaningful, authentic relationships, and leaving lasting impressions with almost anyone you meet (Chapter 6).

5. **Maintaining relationships:** Nurturing and sustaining ongoing connections over time with the right people for you (Chapter 7).

6. **Leveraging your connections for results:** Harnessing your network authentically, to help you achieve tangible outcomes and desired results (Chapter 8).

Living a fulfilled life through relationships: Key principles

Here are a few main principles to remember about living a fulfilled life through relationships.

Skills

Develop authentic, caring connections that draw people in. While everyone has a network, most don't know how to create effective connections that lift them higher. It's about developing the skill to connect genuinely, making those relationships a source of support, fulfillment, and mutual growth. The *Human Factor* Methodology in this book covers the skills enhancement principle.

Opportunities

Connections are the seeds for creating opportunities because 'opportunities come through people'. Knowing how to identify opportunities and make them happen in a way that benefits both parties is a powerful ability.

Timing

Sometimes, even when we are prepared to achieve our goals, challenges related to budget, focus, alignment, or market conditions can arise. Timing plays a crucial role in reaching our objectives. It is essential to understand and navigate these challenges to ensure your efforts align with the right moments.

Giving

Embrace the principle of giving wholeheartedly and with love, without expecting anything in return. True fulfillment in relationships comes from a genuine willingness to give and support others selflessly.

I'll conclude with a quote from Israel's ninth President and visionary, Shimon Peres, who said:

'The future belongs to those who dare to dream and take risks.'

If you wish to live a meaningful life and manifest your goals and dreams, go out there and meet new people, even if it doesn't feel comfortable. By staying proactive, you'll continuously improve in achieving your goals and immensely enrich both your life and the lives of those around you.

Dream big: You can achieve anything you want; I believe in you.

Lirone Glikman

Visit my website to download the workbook for *The Super Connector's Playbook*, to excel in your networking and take your professional and personal life to the next level. Visit: www.lironeglikman.com/TSCPworkbook

Scan me

Connect With Me

Ready to build impactful connèctions? Then it's time to take action! You've reached the end of this book, but your journey to build authentic relationships and transform your network as a master is just beginning. It is time for you to put your learnings into practice and create a network that fulfills your life's goals and supports the people you interact with.

Also, if you have any stories or results from applying the methods in this book, please share them with me; I'm truly eager to learn about your journey.

Connect with me on social media @LironeGlikman on all platforms:

LinkedIn – www.linkedin.com/in/lironeglikman/
Instagram – www.instagram.com/lirone_glikman/
X (Twitter) – twitter.com/lironeglikman
YouTube – www.youtube.com/user/Lironeglikman
TikTok – www.tiktok.com/@glikwoman
Website: www.LironeGlikman.com

Yours,

Lirone Glikman

Author Biography

Lirone Glikman is a globally recognized expert and keynote speaker specializing in business relationships, personal branding, and global business development in a rapidly evolving digital world. She owns *The Human Factor by Lirone Glikman*, a global consultancy and training firm.

Lirone has shared her methodology on business relationships and personal branding in 26+ countries, working with countless professionals and leaders worldwide, from Fortune 500 companies to universities and governments. She also consults for cutting-edge startups on marketing and business development.

With over 20 years of global experience across the U.S., Europe, Australia, and Israel, Lirone regularly writes for leading global business magazines, sharing her knowledge and passion worldwide. She is also an honorary advisor to a United Nations–affiliated NGO committee focused on the Sustainable Development Goals.

Acknowledgments

This book was made with love and is the result of a lifetime of human interactions. I want to thank the special people around me—my family, friends, students, and customers. You have all played a crucial role in helping me design my communication vision and style, and the *Human Factor* methodology. Your influence has been essential in planting the seeds that led to the creation of this book. I'm deeply grateful to have you in my life.

Special thanks to my dear parents, Sima (may her soul rest in peace) and Arie Glikman, my siblings: Guy Glikman and Eva-Tal Glikman, to Rotem, May, Agam, and Or Glikman, Lior Landsman and Yasmin Lahav. Additional thanks to Hadar Matchulsky, Mama Mali Matchulsky (RIP), Penina Weinbach (RIP), Gali Daniel, Danielle Golan, Shay Rokach, Nir Zavaro, Meital Shamia, Nataly Suliman-Shavit, and Dr. John Demartini.

My heartfelt gratitude goes to the Passionpreneur Publishing team, especially to Shobha and Cat, for their shared commitment in bringing this book to life.

Thank you!

Bibliography

American Heart Association (2023). *Thankfulness: How gratitude can help your health.* https://www.heart.org/

Brand Builders Group (2021). *Trends in personal branding.* https://brandbuildersgroup.com/trends/

Brownell, J. (2012). *Listening: Attitudes, principles, and skills* (5th ed.). Allyn & Bacon.

Carnegie, D. (1936). *How to win friends and influence people.* Simon & Schuster.

Cialdini, R.B. (2009). *Influence: The psychology of persuasion* (Rev. ed.). Harper Business.

Clinton, B. (2004). *My life.* Alfred A. Knopf.

Cross, S.E. & Madson, L. (1997). Models of the self: Self-construals and gender. *Psychological Bulletin, 122*(1), 5-37. https://doi.org/10.1037/0033-2909.122.1.5

Dunbar, R.I.M. (2010). *How many friends does one person need? Dunbar's number and other evolutionary quirks.* Faber & Faber.

Eagly, A.H. & Wood, W. (2012). Social role theory. In P.A.M. Van Lange, A.W. Kruglanski & E.T. Higgins (Eds.), *Handbook of theories of social psychology: Volume 2* (pp. 458-476). Sage Publications.

Ferrazzi, K. & Raz, T. (2005). *Never eat alone: And other secrets to success, one relationship at a time.* Currency/Doubleday.

Forleo, M. (2019). *Everything is Figureoutable.* Portfolio.

Franklin, B. (1996). *The autobiography of Benjamin Franklin.* Dover Publications. (Original work published 1791)

Garcia, H. & Miralles, F. (2017). *Ikigai: The Japanese secret to a long and happy life*. Penguin Books.

Goleman, D. (1995). *Emotional intelligence: Why it can matter more than IQ*. Bantam Books.

Gould, R.V. & Fernandez, R.M. (1989). Structures of mediation: A formal approach to brokerage in transaction networks. *Sociological Methodology, 19*, 89-126. https://doi.org/10.2307/270949

Harari, Y.N. (2015). *Sapiens: A brief history of humankind*. Harper.

Huffington, A. (2014). *Thrive: The third metric to redefining success and creating a life of well-being, wisdom, and wonder*. Harmony Books.

Ibarra, H. & Andrews, S.B. (1993). Power, social influence, and sense making: Effects of network centrality and proximity on employee perceptions. *Administrative Science Quarterly, 38*(2), 277-303. https://doi.org/10.2307/2393414

Marsden, P.V. (1987). Core discussion networks of Americans. *American Sociological Review, 52*(1), 122-131. https://doi.org/10.2307/2095397

Milgram, S. (1967). The small-world problem. *Psychology Today, 2*(1), 60-67.

Misner, I., Pollard, S. & Haller, S. (2018). *Who's in your room? The secret to creating your best life*. Indigo River Publishing.

Mogi, K. (2017). *Awakening your Ikigai: How the Japanese wake up to joy and purpose every day*. Experiment.

Orai (2020). *48 fear of public speaking statistics you should know in 2020*. https://www.orai.com/fear-public-speaking-statistics/

Peres, S. (2017). *No room for small dreams: Courage, imagination, and the making of modern Israel*. Custom House.

Petrone, P. (2015). Why referrals are the best source of hire. LinkedIn. https://www.linkedin.com/business/talent/blog/talent-acquisition/reasons-employee-referrals-are-best-way-to-hire

Port, M. (2006). *Book yourself solid: The fastest, easiest, and most reliable system for getting more clients than you can handle even if you hate marketing and selling.* Wiley.

Rogers, C.R. & Farson, R.E. (1957). *Active listening.* University of Chicago, Industrial Relations Center.

Six degrees of Kevin Bacon (2024, August 7). In *Wikipedia.* https://en.wikipedia.org/wiki/Six_Degrees_of_Kevin_Bacon

SpamLaws (2018). *Spam statistics and facts.* https://www.spamlaws.com/spam-stats.html

Tracy, B. (2004). *Power networking: 59 secrets for personal & professional success.* Success Books.

Van Edwards, V. (2017*). Captivate: The science of succeeding with people.* Portfolio/Penguin.

Van Edwards, V. (2022). *Cues: Master the secret language of charismatic communication.* Portfolio.

UCLA Health (2023). *Health benefits of gratitude.* https://www.uclahealth.org/

Wiseman, R. (2003). *The luck factor: The four essential principles.* Miramax Books.

Yello. (n.d.). Research: Why recruiters say referrals are the best talent source. Retrieved from https://yello.co/blog/research-why-recruiters-say-referrals-are-the-best-talent-source/

Ziglar, Z. (2007). *Ziglar on selling: The ultimate handbook for the complete sales professional.* Thomas Nelson.

www.ingramcontent.com/pod-product-compliance
Lightning Source LLC
Chambersburg PA
CBHW040856210326
41597CB00029B/4868